TAUNTON CIDER AND LANGDONS

A West Somerset Story of Industrial Development

TAUNTON CIDER AND LANGDONS

A West Somerset Story of Industrial Development

R.W. Holder

Phillimore

2000

Published by
PHILLIMORE & CO. LTD.
Shopwyke Manor Barn, Chichester, West Sussex

© R.W. Holder, 2000

R.W. Holder has asserted his right under the Copyright, Design and Patent Act,
1988, to be identified as the Author of this work.

ISBN 1 86077 137 8

Printed and bound in Great Britain by
BOOKCRAFT LTD.
Midsomer Norton

CONTENTS

An Explanation

In 1956 the late Mr F. Graham Clark wrote a short book entitled *A Somerset Life— An Account of the Business Career of Mrs. B.A. Langdon of Wiveliscombe*. He told the story of a business which had been established first in a small town in west Somerset, and then also in Taunton, through the enterprise of a farmer's daughter called Bessie Hill, who married a saddler called Thomas Langdon. Under successive owners, the firm, which is still called Langdons, has survived and grown. Its Commercial Director, Rob Swindells, thought it would be interesting to the company's employees and customers, as well as good publicity, to bring the story up to date. He asked me to do the job.

After talking to those involved, reading local histories, and seeing many published and unpublished documents, I decided to do more than write a standard company history or hagiography. The relationship between Langdons and the company which grew into Taunton Cider plc became very close. When I started delving into the past, I inevitably became intrigued by what happened to Taunton Cider plc, and why. I therefore decided to tell that story as well. I have to thank the cider experts who have helped me with the relevant chapters. The facts are the facts but the comments are mine.

Going back to the origins of both companies in the 19th century, the Rectors of Heathfield and the farmer's daughter from Wiveliscombe were only able to establish their businesses because of the distribution network of the Great Western Railway, as it was to become. To fill in that background, I decided to record the development of communications from and around Taunton: the Navigation of the River Tone, the Turnpikes, the Bridgwater and Taunton Canal, the Railway Age, and then the effect of the internal combustion engine and road traffic. This may be of more interest to local people than to any general reader but I suspect the same kind of evolution happened all over the country. Change the name of the town, the canal or river, the railway company, and the motorway, and the story would be much the same.

I was also reminded of the effect outside events have on the development or decline of businesses. It would, for example, be difficult to explain to a modern reader why Langdons did not return to the transport business for long after the end of the Second World War without noting the nationalisation of road haulage. In addition I have referred to other external factors such as the development of the motor vehicle, the two World Wars, the General Strike, the Great Depression, the industrial problems of the 1960s and 1970s, and the regulation of the brewing industry. I also tell of specific incidents where intrusive regulation and excessive zeal on the part of public servants has affected the creation of wealth for the community as a whole.

While there are hundreds of books about the railways, I know of none which explains to the layman how modern logistic firms work. With the railways effectively out of the entrepôt market, society relies totally on road transport for its food, its fuel, and virtually every other product. With this in mind, I have taken the opportunity of explaining how road transport and distribution has evolved, using Langdons as my example. The industry would be even more efficient, and produce even more wealth, if it were better understood by those whose duty it is to provide an adequate infrastructure and if our taxation policy on Heavy Goods Vehicles and diesel fuel conformed more closely with that of our European partners and competitors.

Writing this book has also taught me much about the development of the county town near which I have lived for nearly fifty years. Taunton evolved as a manufacturing and market town. Its leaders, through their planning policies, have sought to turn it into a residential and administrative centre. There is occasional talk of 'attracting new industry' but those who have been involved in economic development know that it is more important, and rewarding, to foster what you already have, and provide places where local people can start new businesses, than to try to attract the footloose, who may or may not stay. Of the three larger companies for which I have worked locally, Avimo had to go to appeal twice before expanding in Taunton, building in Barnstaple while it wasted two years. James Pearsall were able to build a new factory because they did so on Crown land, where the Queen doesn't have to obtain planning permission. And Langdons in 1999 had to move the heart of its operation to Bridgwater.

I offer my thanks to the many people who have given me information about both Taunton Cider and about Langdons. I also express my gratitude to my editor, Dr. Michael Allen, who has helped in many ways with advice and support, and to Mr. Kenneth Steel, who drew the map.

West Monkton
September 2000

One

How Transport and Communications Developed in West Somerset

TAUNTON *(Tone-ton)*, so named for being built on the banks of the river Tone, is situated in the extensive and beautiful valley of Taunton Deane, or vale of Taunton, in the county of Somerset, 44 miles south-west of Bristol by railway. It communicates by railway with the Bristol and English channels. The streets are wide, well-paved and lighted; the shops are modern and capacious, but the woollen and silk factories which were once extensive here have almost wholly departed ...

Ina, king of the West Saxons, built a castle in T. about 700 A.D. This was soon after destroyed, but another fortress was built on the site soon after the Conquest, at which period the town had a mint ...

To T. Castle, Perkin Warbeck fled when he failed in storming Exeter. During the civil wars between Charles and the parliament, the town was twice besieged by Goring, but twice successfully defended by Colonel Blake. In T. Monmouth received the heartiest welcome, and Judge Jeffreys exercised his unbounded cruelty.

Chambers's Encyclopaedia (1874), Vol.IX, pp.314-15

Taunton is the county town of Somerset, the place where people 'come up from' and 'the cider apples grow'. The contributor to *Chambers's* in the 1874 edition understood the importance of transport because he tells us about its communication with the rest of the world by railway before moving on to its turbulent history and other attractions. The railway still runs through the town, providing a frequent and rapid service to London in particular. However, both with goods and people, most of the traffic into, out of and past the town is by road. Lots of books have been written about the Somerset railways, and a few about its canals. Here our attention will be directed rather to road transport, looking at it through the experiences of two local companies, Langdons, who are hauliers, and the manufacturer Taunton Cider. As both firms started life in the railway age, we can follow how the transition from rail to road affected their development and the local economy.

The principal highway through Somerset and past Taunton is the M5 motorway. It enters the county from the north-east after circling round Bristol. The scenery offers nothing special as the road sweeps mile after mile across the flat and often windswept Somerset Levels, with interesting places like Cheddar or the Mendips away to the left, and the Quantocks a distant skyline to the right. The observant passengers will notice the drainage ditches and reflect that the land through which they are passing, like a third of the county, lies below sea level, kept dry all the year round by pumping, and even then liable to flood in winter. The historian may thank King Charles for giving his favourite, the Duke of Buckingham, permission to drain the Levels, although as he traverses Sedgemoor he will see no trace of the battlefield where Charles's grandson, the Duke of Monmouth, came to grief. The marshes of this land gave King Alfred refuge from the Danes. It was here that he founded our first nunnery and made his name for generations of schoolchildren as a careless cook. Alfred also introduced English as a written language alongside Latin, but inevitably it is those burnt cakes for which he seems to be best remembered.

The motorway itself posed major engineering problems because much of it rests on peat. For the same reason, many of the incongruous warehouse buildings at the intersections have needed piling to a depth of 40 feet. Rushing past junction 25, the congested access to Taunton, there is little to make the passer-by reflect on the part geography and the Levels have played in the development of the county town and of west Somerset. Those who stray off the motorway towards Taunton find a settlement which looks much like anywhere else these days—out-of-town superstores, a few fine old buildings and streets, plenty of charity shops, building societies, beggars and banks, pubs and multiples, too many cars and not enough parking spaces; as for the motorway itself—no different from any other, except for a plethora of cones and lane closures while it is constantly under repair because of its soggy bed.

Surrounded on three sides by marshes, Taunton was an Anglo-Saxon rather than a Roman settlement, the Romano-British having colonised what is now the village of Norton Fitzwarren on rising ground some three miles to the west of the town. We shall hear more about Norton Fitzwarren later, because that was the home of the Taunton Cider Company and of a military supply base from the Second World War. If the Romans had been able to lay one of their straight roads across the fens, Norton Fitzwarren and Taunton might have been afforded a direct route to London. Because that was not an option, Taunton remains to this day unique as a county town in having no direct road to the capital, and even the journey to Bristol was circuitous until the Levels had been drained. It may be that this comparative isolation contributed to the warm reception the townspeople gave to Perkin Warbeck, Blake, the Duke of Monmouth and any other rebels against central government who came their way.

Because of the difficulty in transporting and storing food and fuel in the winter, or what we would now call by the jargon word logistics, there was, prior to the Railway Age, only one settlement in England of more than three thousand people which was not connected with some form of water-borne transport—river, sea or canal. (The exception was Luton, made unusually prosperous by its manufacture of hats.) For four months of the year, if townspeople couldn't move traffic by water, they couldn't use the roads either to carry any significant volume of food or fuel because they were impassable except for light vehicles, pack horses or porters. We can still see here and there the ledges on which the weary carrier could rest his load off his back, like the one in Piccadilly in London. We can guess the state of the roads in winter around Taunton from the sunken lanes of today. Iron wheels on the horse-drawn carts wore deep ruts until the middle of the road snagged the axles, after which the surface was levelled by removing the earth from the ridge in the middle, and the process started over again.

In 1752 the Taunton Turnpike Trust was established—the term Public/Private Initiative had yet to be coined—and gradually the roads leading into the town were drained, paved and otherwise improved, with special attention being given to the Great London Road. Fifty years later the coach from Taunton to London took two days rather than four as previously and by 1822 the time had been reduced to just under

24 hours, although that was probably a freak, rather like driving from Taunton to Heathrow today on the M4 without becoming held up in a traffic jam. If we keep our eyes open, we can still see a few toll houses in the county, many converted into rather twee roadside cottages.

Despite the improvement to the roads, when more than three thousand souls gathered in one settlement without water-borne access, with over three thousand mouths to feed and bodies to warm, supplies failed and the poorer people froze and starved. This happened throughout England on the eve of the Railway Age in the 'Hungry Forties', when an increase in population, the delayed repeal of the Corn Laws, and potato blight formed a deadly combination throughout rural England, although less deadly than in Ireland.

Taunton was able to grow beyond the critical number of three thousand inhabitants because it lay astride the river Tone which was navigable, first as far as Langport, then to Ham, a village some three miles short of the town where a mill had been built soon after 1325, and eventually in the early 16th century to the town itself. Every stage of the journey was difficult for a boat. The Bristol Channel, with its 40-foot tides, has on the south side no natural harbour. The twisting journey on the Parrett up-river through the mud banks to Bridgwater depended on the tides, as indeed did the barges and tubs through to Langport itself. There were advantages in having your port some way inland like Bridgwater, or Bristol, where it was less likely to be attacked by marauders. As late as 20 June 1631 Baltimore in County Cork was raided by North African pirates who sacked the town and carried away 111 prisoners, leaving the survivors to found a safer place to live inland at Skibbereen.

The raid on Baltimore was a material influence on Charles when he introduced the notorious tax, Ship Money, partly to meet for his own expenses, but also to strengthen his navy against such piracy in future. Nowhere was the tax less popular than in the rebellious vale of Taunton Deane, the populist William Prynne and the parliamentary leader John Pym both being Somerset men. In nearby Wellington in 1640, mutinous soldiers lynched their officer, while the townspeople looked on with approval. Even Sir William Portman, the aristocratic member of parliament for Taunton, came out against the king, although, like so many others in the county, he was to rally to the royal cause later.

As urban populations grew, more and more woodland was felled to provide fuel, both for the home and for industrial purposes such as lime-burning or the smithy. Faced with this deforestation, an alternative fuel to wood had to be found, and, for west Somerset, coal from Wales provided the answer. In 1638 John Malet, the Sheriff of Somerset, obtained a Commission under the Great Seal of Charles to improve the Tone for the carriage of goods, mainly coal, as far as Ham Mills near Taunton. Malet may have thought he was on to a good thing, being authorised to levy a toll for the use of the river, but the work proved more of a burden than he had anticipated, and was incomplete when he died. His son took on the task without making much progress. When the son in turn died in 1656, his sister took over, and then her children. In the end the scale of the works involved proved too big for any individual to finance, and the continuing bad state of the river began to threaten Taunton's prosperity. This was not just of concern to the merchants of the town. Excessive freight costs feed through immediately to the cost of goods, affecting everyone's standard of living, with the poor suffering most. It is a lesson which politicians, who see taxes on fuel as an easy option, find only too easy to forget.

In 1697, 34 Taunton traders and merchants met to discuss the unsatisfactory state of the river, which was damaging their businesses. Their initiative resulted eventually in the navigation being taken over by a statutory body entitled the Conservators of the River Tone, consisting of local worthies. The Conservators continue in a ceremonial role to this day, election to their number being jealously guarded against newcomers, or what the Irish felicitously call blow-ins. Thanks to the enterprise and efforts of the early Conservators, and their money, by the start of the 19th century the river was as good as it was likely to get, despite its flooding, its weirs, its mills and its sandbanks. For all the improvements, delays of up to seven hours were commonplace for a barge, especially if there was a drought and a miller was being greedy about releasing water. Few river navigations were efficient enough to survive the Canal Age, and the Tone certainly wasn't one of them.

Bridgwater port, some 11 miles from Taunton as the crow flies but a lot further away by water, had developed considerably by the 1820s, handling cargoes from abroad as well as the local trade in coal and bricks. There was the usual, and unusually well-documented, dickering about the construction of a canal from Bridgwater to Taunton which continued for a decade or more, which shows that things haven't changed much when it comes to making decisions about improving the transport infrastructure, who-ever is financing it. The work eventually started in 1824 and the canal was opened to Taunton in January 1827, to be greeted with enthusiasm by the inhabitants, who would have relished any occasion where there was plenty of free food and drink. Among them many must have reflected that improved communication would increase the prosperity of the town: as indeed it should, and did, and does.

You may remember the fuss there was when the Bristol Aeroplane Company developed the Brabazon airliner—the 'Whispering Giant' and all that. Unfortunately its certification coincided with the arrival of the jet age, and the whisper soon changed to an embarrassed silence. So it was with most of the canals when the railways came, and especially with the Bridgwater and Taunton, although the profligacy of its proprietors was to hasten its failure.

Old pictures show just how congested the natural harbour in Bridgwater had become by the 1830s, and the canal proprietors engaged Thomas Maddicks to build for them a new basin, with a new canal cut to Huntworth, some two miles out of town, for the sum of £25,000. Unfortunately for them, the work cost £100,000. To add to their woes, the original canal had only been open just over nine years when, on 19 May 1836, the Bristol and Exeter Railway Company secured an Act of Parliament for the construction of a line from Temple Meads in Bristol to 'meadows in the Parish of St Thomas' in Exeter, passing through Bridgwater and Taunton. In March 1840 the railway's franchise was taken over by the Great Western Railway, and in June 1842 the line was opened to Taunton, reaching the Devon border in 1843. That same year, 1842, the canal company opened a connecting canal to Chard, with a view to linking eventually the Bristol and English channels by water. Although the Taunton to Chard railway, which made the Chard canal redundant, was not operational until 1860, the loss of business to the railway between Bridgwater and Taunton combined with the overspending on the new dock pushed the canal company into receivership, where it remained for some years.

There was only one buyer. The Great Western needed the water in the canal, to use both in its steam engines and to flush out regularly the dock in Bridgwater.

Eventually, in 1866, the receivers sold the canal to the Great Western Railway. The other canals radiating from Taunton, to Chard and to Tiverton, passed out of use. As a condition of buying the Bridgwater and Taunton Canal, the Great Western had to give the normal undertakings about continued competition which are expected of a monopoly when it needs government approval to drive a competitor out of business, but that did not prevent it doing as little as it could get away with in the way of keeping the waterway open. It was left for the army in 1940 to make the cut completely impassable when they turned the line of the canal into a tank barrier, festooning its banks with pillboxes.

Taunton quickly took to being a railway town. There was still no main road to London, and the GWR became known as the Great Way Round, because of the need to travel to the capital city through Bristol and Swindon from Taunton and stations west. In July 1906 trains were able to go direct to London from Taunton via Westbury, making a rare example of a line developed in the Motor Age not having to deviate to pick up customers from small towns and villagers near its route. It was not until 1932 that this line was engineered to its present high standard.

With the Bristol to Exeter line completed, branches from Taunton quickly extended in all directions. Apart from the access to Bristol and to Exeter, and (much later) the Westbury direct route to London, other tracks ran to Yeovil, Chard, Minehead and Barnstaple, passing through and having stations in many small towns and villages on their way.

The Devon & Somerset Railway secured its Act for a line from Taunton to Barnstaple on 29 June 1864, leaving the main line at Norton Fitzwarren. The railway reached Wiveliscombe, 13 miles from Taunton on 8 June 1871, after the work had been held up by a major labour dispute and an epidemic of cholera. This line continued to carry freight until August 1954, and passenger traffic until 3 October 1966. Despite the emotional cries for its retention, the economic case against it was compelling. I came back from Barnstaple to Taunton by train one evening in 1959. There were five of us aboard from Swimbridge, near Barnstaple, to Milverton, the next station between Wiveliscombe and Taunton: the driver, the fireman, the guard, another man and me. There were no goods in the guard's van.

Wiveliscombe is a small town, set in farming country on the edge of Exmoor. Before the railway came, it had the typical self-sufficiency of a country town with no more than road communication to the outside world. The assizes were held in Taunton, but Wiveliscombe had its own Magistrates' Court, and its own policemen. It had a market, medical resources, schools, shops, a bank, tradesmen. It also had a famous brewery, Arnold and Hancock, with the Hancock family living in a mansion on the edge of town and doing good works, apart from the supply of beer, which is considered another good work by many of us.

As throughout the country, the coming of the railway ended Wiveliscombe's isolation, genetically and commercially. The average distance in which a marriage partner was selected went from under five miles to over forty, giving a chance at last to breed out some of those regressive genes which caused so many rural Somerset infants to be 'changed'. (The malevolent fairies did the 'changing', turning a bonny baby into a half-wit or making it grow up deformed. The parents, often closely related, were of course blameless.) Arnold and Hancock's beers took on the mighty Starkey, Knight and Ford of Bridgwater over a wide area. Cattle no longer had to spend days walking the drove-roads, and losing weight which the drover would try to compensate by feeding salt, on the way to the slaughterhouse. Rabbits, milk, eggs, butter and other produce could be sent to Bristol or London daily. Coal replaced wood in almost every stove and hearth. Most people didn't take holidays, but for the Sunday School treat or the special day, there was an excursion to Woolacombe (change at Barnstaple and walk from Mortehoe unless you took the one train a day over the mixed broad and narrow gauge to Ilfracombe), or to the metropolis of Taunton. The railway seemed to have a dominance and reach, and a permanence, which the canals could never achieve. It seemed omnipotent, indispensable, indestructible.

Despite the railway, life on the farms, where most country people lived and worked, changed less than for the townspeople. Farmers, farm-workers and their families were used to having no electricity, gas, piped water or main drainage. Fuel wasn't a problem because there was plenty of wood for the fire, and fodder for the horses. For the farmer, bills were run up on an annual basis with tradesmen and shopkeepers, and settled after the harvest. You killed your own pork and lambs, grew your own vegetables, cut your own wood and brewed your own cider. Wages and earnings were low but you ate the food you grew, and grew the wood you burned. The boys would find a job on a farm, and the girls in service, until they married, when most of them benefited from having learned the rudiments of cooking and housekeeping despite the long hours and low pay which they had experienced.

Then came the internal combustion engine, which takes us back to the M5 motorway, and the motorists rushing past junction 25, not noticing the Bridgwater and Taunton Canal as they twice pass over it, but perhaps racing a train on the old Exeter and Bristol stretch between Bridgwater and Highbridge. They can hardly miss the gigantic signs between Taunton and Bridgwater, **LANGDONS**, advertising the lorry parks and warehouses. The name takes us back to Mrs. Bessie Langdon née Hill, a farmer's daughter, and to Wiveliscombe, where she lived. Mrs. Langdon (we wouldn't dare use her Christian name once she was married) was born on a farm in Huish Champflower, a small west Somerset village, in 1881. What follows is partly her story, and partly about cider. It is also a story of how developments in transport and distribution have changed our towns and villages, and our countryside, and our lives and habits, and ourselves.

Two

HOW THE RECTORS OF HEATHFIELD STARTED
COMMERCIAL CIDER-MAKING

To maintain some semblance of chronological order, we have to delay delving into the antecedents of Langdons, whose warehouses stand beside the M5, and whose gleaming white tractors and articulated trailers, with their blue logos, catch our eye on our travels, once we start looking out for them. As we have already noted, Somerset and cider are closely associated in the public mind, just as love and marriage used to be. The brand name everyone knows is that of *Taunton Cider*, although, as we will learn in due course, the cider so named is no longer made in Taunton and latterly a minority of its constituent apples grew in Somerset. In due time we shall attend the marriage between the manufacturer, Taunton Cider, and its principal haulier and distributor, Langdons, and, later, study the divorce. First however we must look at how a commercial cider industry developed near Taunton in the first place.

Apple trees thrive in much the same areas as vines. They especially like the west country, with its mild winters and its generous rainfall. Of all the alcoholic drinks, cider is among the simplest to make, requiring no more than apples and patience: Mrs. Beeton's instructions are as easy to follow as when she wrote them, and the result from the first pressing of selected apples without any additives can be both potent and delicious. The second pressing produces a less intoxicating drink, and was much favoured in the summer where the normal agricultural labourer's ration of three or four pints a day might be increased to six or eight during harvest time. A German scientist named Voelcker analysed this 'small cider' issued to farm workers in the mid-19th century in Somerset and found that, if undiluted with water, it had an alcoholic content of 4 per cent. It is small wonder that, even after the Second World War, half the patients of Tone Vale mental hospital near Taunton were men who had habitually drunk up to 24 pints of cider a day at a cost of no more than 4d. a pint. Most of the other half were third-degree syphilitic patients: we had not in those days abandoned caring for aged or simple relatives within the family, or consigned mentally ill people to the ministrations of public servants.

For those with no apple trees of their own, the practice was to gather windfalls or the remainder of the crop which the owner of the orchard could not be bothered to pick, 'scrumping' them, as it was called in Somerset. The resulting cider might be rougher than a first pressing of choice apples, but, for a labourer, a supply of 'scrumpy' was better than no liquor at all. Because the drink was so easy to make, apples plentiful and transport poor, cider was usually drunk in the immediate area of its production, with householders and cider houses buying from local farmers. The drink was said 'not to travel well', probably because each district became accustomed to the taste of cider from its local types of tree, and rejected flavours favoured in another district. Everyone with spare apples made cider, even men of the cloth.

The late 18th and early 19th centuries gave the nation a clerical profession which, in the countryside at least, was better off than anyone other than the squire. The Napoleonic Wars, by restricting imports, saw huge increases in the price of grain, which benefited landowners and farmers but caused hardship if not starvation among the poor.

Such favourable trading conditions were not lightly to be given up when the wars ended at Waterloo in 1815. The inflated prices which had obtained during the twenty years of conflict and blockade were perpetuated by Corn Laws which, like the Common Agricultural Policy today, ensured that farmers secured higher prices for their produce than would obtain under free trade, and so for landowners higher rents from the farmers. The townsman and the poor who had to pay the cost of all this had no political voice before the Reform Act of 1832, and it would be another ten years before the squirearchy's stranglehold on food prices was finally loosened.

The system benefited not only the farmer and the landowner: the parson, with his tithe, or tenth, and his glebe, rode along on their coat-tails. When people talked of an incumbent enjoying 'a good living', that was no more than a statement of an economic truth. We are fortunate in still being able to follow the fortunes of the Brontë family at Haworth, when we can contrast the difference between the lifestyle of the shepherd and that of his flock. A 'living' also left enough money for the incumbent to pay a curate to do the Lord's work for him.

So too it was in Heathfield, a parish of fertile farmland in Taunton Deane bordering on Norton Fitzwarren. The Rector not only enjoyed a comfortable lifestyle with plenty of servants to attend his needs and those of his family; he also farmed and profited from a handsome glebe, and a glebe planted with Kingston Black apples, from which particularly delicious cider was made. Naturally there was no question of the rector himself doing the menial tasks associated with the gathering of the crop or the pressing of the fruit, although successive holders of the holy office showed an interest in the art which was not merely pecuniary. Under their pastoral care Heathfield Rectory cider acquired a reputation for quality which grew rapidly beyond the parochial boundary.

The incumbent in the 1820s and 1830s was clearly a man whose choice of profession was a gain to the church and a loss to the world of business. We cannot be sure when he started marketing his cider more widely but that had certainly happened before the repeal of the Corn Laws in 1842. Later Heathfield rectory cider would be exhibited at those exhibitions of which the Victorians were so fond, winning gold and silver medals along with national acclaim.

The first surviving record of the trade carried on at Heathfield by the Reverend Thomas Cornish is a receipt from June 1842 recording the sale of a hogshead of cider to St James's Palace in London at a price of £10 3s. 0d. The size of a hogshead depended to some extent on its contents, whether beer, wine, or cider, and on the cooper's whim. A good guess would be that the one sold to the Palace contained some 54 imperial gallons, or whatever the equivalent is in litres. There is a further note, also dated 1842, to the effect that the debt owing from the Reform Club would not be received until after it had audited its accounts in November. No doubt, with its complement of archbishops and bishops, deans and the presenters of livings among the membership, the Reverend Mr. Cornish was not inclined to press the Club too hard for payment.

Two factors had enabled successive rectors to expand their market beyond Taunton Deane and the west country. The first was the rail service, and the second the much improved rapidity of communication when letters were carried by train rather than by mail coach. Mr. Cornish's surviving 'Cellar Book' was kept meticulously from 1843 to 1865 and illustrates the extent to which the railway had created commercial opportunities, and the avidity with which he and others had seized them. In the summer there would be a dozen to sixteen shipments of cider a month and, taking a sample of those outside the immediate vicinity, the following are recorded from a typical period in 1843:

Sir Richard Simeon	Isle of Wight	via GWR
W. Dell	Aylesbury	via Paddington
Viscount Melbourne	Grosvenor Square*	
Thomas Brand	Burlington House,	Piccadilly*
William Cavendish	Burlington House, Piccadilly*	
George Collins	Wisbeach	by ship
John Spurway	Lower Crescent, Bath*	
Francis Chorley	Leeds*	
James Giles	Croydon, Surrey*	
Sir Henry Bayly	Lyme Regis	by waggon
Richard Stothert	Hay Hill House, Bath*	
Lady Mount Edgcumbe	Plymouth	(GWR to Exeter, then by a Topsham trader to Plymouth)
G.P. Dawson	Osgodby Hall, Selby, Yorks*	
Lord Kinnaird	Rossie Priory, Dundee	

The entries I have marked with an asterisk would almost certainly have recorded deliveries of cider by rail in addition to those where the railway is mentioned, like those to Sir Richard Simeon on the Isle of Wight and to Mr. Dell. Then, as now, communications across the peninsula remained poor, resulting in Sir Henry Bayly's delivery to Lyme Regis by road. As Brunel was not to open his South Devon Railway to Plymouth until 1848, following his brave but unsuccessful atmospheric experiment, Lady Mount Edgcumbe had to rely for her supply on a carter westward from Exeter. There was a rail link to Dundee, but the shipment to Lord Kinnaird may well have gone by sea, like that to Wisbech (for which the Revd Cornish preferred an alternative spelling). The Cellar Book is also instructive in showing the eminence of the customers for what we might have considered a plebeian drink. On the other hand, with carriage to be paid, only the rich could afford the luxury of going into the market for a quality product when that produced locally was so cheap.

The Revd Cornish eventually gave way as rector to the Spurway family, the last of the line being the Revd Edward Spurway, who was as concerned with the cider-making as with his other duties and even emulated Voelcker by introducing a hydrometer to test the specific gravity of the cider. By 1910, the Heathfield Rectory under his management was producing some 5,000 gallons of cider a year, which was sold to the great and the good throughout the land. The rectory curtilage had become the home of an industrial unit with milling and pressing machinery, a fermenting cellar and a bottling plant. Then in 1912 Edward Spurway fell ill and the business was for two years or so sadly neglected. After his death his successor, the Revd Guy Hockley, declined to regenerate the business and gave up commercial cider-making, no doubt being quite properly more interested in the cure of souls than the pleasures of the flesh.

At this juncture a Milverton builder, William Vickery, appeared on the scene. According to local legend, he had seen hogsheads of cider in the rectory gardens awaiting delivery by the Revd Spurway, and thought that it looked a better business to be in than building. The rector, Mr. Hockley, sold him the orchards and some of the equipment, no doubt glad to be free of any association with the demon drink. Vickery must have hoped to pick up the goodwill of the business and recover its eminent clientele, but he seems to have had little of the commercial acumen of his clerical predecessors. Knowing nothing of the cider-maker's art, he offered a job to the rector's head gardener, who had doubled as cider-maker, but preferred, patrioti-cally if unwisely, to answer Kitchener's call to arms. The under-gardener, Arthur Moore, also knew the secrets such as they were, and went into partnership with Vickery to restart cider production from the Heathfield apples in new premises in Norton Fitzwarren.

Meanwhile a business in Rickmansworth which also made cider, along with bottled water, minerals, pickles and chutney, was being sold by its owner Daniel Pallett to the Idris company, one of the conditions of sale being that Daniel and his son George, who was also in the business, did not re-start trading in competition with Idris. As Mrs. George Pallett hailed from Somerset, George and his family decided to return there from Hertfordshire. Some time early in the First World War, George found himself in Norton Fitzwarren with time on his hands, money in his pocket, and some unused knowledge about the cider business. Vickery and Moore had not proved worthy suc-cessors of the rectors of Heathfield when it came to business affairs and were happy to sell their tiny business to Pallett, with Moore remaining for five years as cider-maker before finally emigrating to Australia, after two business ventures in Taunton, one of which, improbably, involved a skating-rink.

By 1919, with the wartime demand for any alcoholic drink at an end, George Pallett also himself found himself in financial difficulty and appealed for help to his former auditor at Rickmansworth, a London accountant called Frank Rowley. Within two years, Rowley had put the finances of the business on a sounder footing and in 1921, Pallett's Cider became the Taunton Cider Company Ltd, with Rowley as its Chairman, Pallett as its Managing Director, six employees in all, and a production of 10,000 gallons a year, or only twice what the rector of Heathfield had been producing less than a decade previously.

Mr. Rowley's accountancy practice had among its clientele several London theatre companies. This stage connection had led him into becoming a theatrical 'angel' and allowed him to introduce Taunton Cider into many crush bars in the theatres with which he was connected. He also opened a fashionable cider-only bar in that theatrical home-from-home, Brighton. Although he never equalled the feat of one of his clerical predecessors, who had shipped a hogshead of cider to the queen and to her Prime Minister on the same day, Frank Rowley was to prove, in his way, as dynamic an entrepreneur as Mrs. Bessie Langdon two stops down the line in Wiveliscombe, and to keep our narrative in some kind of order, we must put the clock back again and introduce her into the story.

Three

WHY A WIVELISCOMBE FARMER'S DAUGHTER
WENT INTO BUSINESS

In June 1897, Bessie Hill, of Ridge Farm, Wiveliscombe, was 15 years old. She had of course left school, but at the age of 12 she had won a prize worth £5, a considerable amount of money then, two weeks' wages for a workman and enough to buy herself a pony. Like all farmers' daughters, she led a busy life with various tasks around the house and yard. Those were still the days when jobs were divided into those which only women could do, like bearing and feeding children: those that women were better at, like looking after young children, sewing, cooking and caring for the home: and those which required physical strength over long hours outdoors, which called for a masculine physique. Society had to wait many decades for legislation to alter that unsatisfactory state of affairs.

Another part of 'women's work' on a farm was tending to the poultry. It was quite common for children, and girls especially, to have their own pet lambs (abandoned by their ewes and hand-reared in the house) or poultry, through which they could earn pocket money. Bessie followed the common pattern by keeping a flock of hens, and selling her eggs to a grocer in Wiveliscombe to whom she delivered them.

One hot afternoon, Bessie collected the eggs and went to harness her pony to pull the trap for the short ride into town. Goods were counted in dozens in those days, the number twelve being more convenient than ten when it came to division: a half, a third, a quarter, a sixth - they all left a whole number, so much more practical than tens, fives and twos. A gross, twelve twelves, was the common unit of commercial reckoning. A gross of eggs weighs heavy, especially on a warm summer's day, and that was the quantity Bessie had collected to sell to the grocer. Unfortunately for her, the pony was already busy pulling a hay-rake for her father, who declined to release it to its owner. If she wanted to sell her eggs, which wouldn't keep too well in the hot weather, Bessie would have to carry them on foot the two miles into Wivesliscombe. And that is what she did.

Hot, dusty, aching, Bessie arrived at the grocer's to be told that he already had a surfeit of eggs. Despite having a cellar, there was a limit to the time he could hold surplus stock before they went off. The best price he could give Bessie for her gross was five shillings. (A shilling being also duodecimal in having twelve pence, it was easy to work out that this amounted to fivepence a dozen. Duodecimal maths was not without its advantages.) It would be simplistic to say that 'five shillings' amounts to 25 pence in today's money, when inflation and vast improvements in living standards have made such comparisons unreal. Rather let us say that five shillings would have bought a boy twenty haircuts, or a man ten: or paid for a room with full board in a medium class hotel for a day: or a live-in maid's wages for a week. It was not a derisory sum, but it wasn't enough to repay feeding the hens, collecting the eggs, and then carrying heavy baskets all the way into town on a stifling June afternoon, and walking home again.

Bessie's father had a better arrangement for marketing his butter. There were five trains a day on the Barnstaple line passing through Wiveliscombe to Taunton; they traversed the bleak emptiness of Exmoor, and stopped for nine minutes at Morebath Junction in the middle of nowhere for the convenience of any passengers wishing to find their way to Bampton, Tiverton and Exeter. The evening, or 'Parliamentary' train, with its controlled fares, left Wivesliscombe at 7.29 and took 22 minutes for the journey to Taunton, stopping at Milverton and Norton Fitzwarren en route. Another Parliamentary train left Taunton at 8.18, reaching Temple Meads at 10.15. There were trains which did the 43 miles to Bristol in half that time, but Parliamentaries had to stop at every halt and station on the way. Using these services, farmer Hill's butter went regularly by rail to a provision merchant, Jesse Watkins, in Bristol, who paid him a better price than if he sold it in Wiveliscombe.

Disappointed at the poor offer for her eggs from the Wiveliscombe grocer, as soon as she arrived home Bessie sat down and wrote to Jesse Watkins, asking him if he would handle her eggs as well as her father's butter. She sent her letter off the same day, although it is not recorded whether she had to walk back to town to post it; but that wouldn't have bothered her. Everyone was used to walking miles in those days. Mr. Watkins replied by return saying he would be a buyer of her eggs at ninepence a dozen so long as they were individually wrapped in newspaper and packed in egg boxes which he would supply. The first consignment went up within a hamper with the butter, to be followed by regular deliveries in the sturdy boxes. Bessie was in business.

At the start, Mr. Watkins was not fussed about the number of eggs he took, which was as well because hens do not lay at an even rate throughout the year. He did, however, have a demand which went far beyond what Bessie's hens could produce. She therefore started taking the output from other farmers' wives and daughters, charging a penny for every dozen eggs she handled for them. At that rate of commission, she cannot have done much collecting, or made much profit. But she was providing a service, and earning good pocket money. So things continued for a decade, with the egg business being only part of Bessie's life on the farm. Then, in 1907, she married a Wiveliscombe saddler called Thomas Richard Langdon, and from now on we must call her Mrs. Langdon.

A decade earlier, in 1896, the repeal of the Highways Act of 1865 had permitted the use of a motor vehicle on a public highway without its being preceded by a man on foot carrying a red flag. Prior to the repeal, the speed of road vehicles in Britain had been limited to four miles an hour in the country, and two in towns, the man with the flag walking 20 yards ahead. Self-propelled steam road vehicles had first been seen in the late 18th century, and had achieved a remarkable degree of reliability, as was demonstrated by Sir Goldsworthy Gurney in 1829 when he drove one from London to Bath and back at an average speed of 15 miles an hour. They remained unpopular, expensive, and noisy: dangerous too, with so many thatched cottages at the roadside and cinders flying from the smokestack. To this day it is forbidden under some model by-laws to build a wooden roof within 60 feet of a highway because of the danger caused by steam lorries and traction engines. (Yes, I know there aren't any steam lorries and traction engines these days, nor have there been for fifty years, but we are dealing with local and national government here, not with organisations which eliminate redundant regulations or forgo an opportunity to control the populace. Power once gained must never be wantonly surrendered.)

The steam car was never going to be much more than a rich man's toy. For one thing, you had to have someone to stoke the engine, or in French the *chauffeur*, or warmer. You also needed a 'chauffeuse', or footwarmer, in your unheated car in cold weather. Solid tyres and bad roads made for an uncomfortable ride, even if the machine wasn't rattled to bits. Horses bolted at the approach of the steaming monster and contemporary cartoons reveal the mirth with which most of these contraptions were viewed. The petrol driven engine quickly changed all that.

The essential development of the internal combustion engine took place in the 1880s, mainly in Germany, France and Austria, where Karl Benz, Gottlieb Daimler, Nicolas Otto, René Panhard, Albert de Dion, Rudolf Diesel and others were tumbling over each other in their innovations, the sum of which resulted in the road vehicles we know today. It was not that British engineers in the 19th century lacked flair and application. The contrary was true, as the development of railway technology and virtually every other branch of engineering showed. There was, however, little incentive for them to put time and money into developing a vehicle which the law said could only be used in conjunction with the man with the red flag. British industrialists are habituated to working in a society where enterprise is stifled and progress blocked by the ignorance or cowardice of politicians. Only Frederick Lanchester, with the propeller shaft and worm drive to the back axle, and Percy Riley, with his mechanically operated valves, made any British significant contribution to the development of the motor vehicle. Herbert Austin and William (Nuffield) Morris were to appear on the scene much later.

Throughout the century and unhampered by political restriction, British highway engineers, inspired by Thomas Telford and John McAdam, constructed roads on which vehicles could travel freely throughout the year. The Irish veterinary surgeon, Dunlop, and the Michelin brothers invented the pneumatic tyres to smooth the bumps. Certainly the early cars would be followed by clouds of dust in summer, as soon as they moved off the few metalled roads, but they were not slow in achieving an acceptable degree of reliability, provided the 'chauffeur'—now without a shovel—was adept at repairing punctures.

In retrospect, it is remarkable how quickly the motor car achieved an acceptable level of reliability. Very few could afford the exquisite and dependable 7-litre Silver Ghost developed by Charles Rolls and Henry Royce in 1906. It was the American Ransome Olds rather than the Irish protestant from Cork, Henry Ford, who first tumbled to the fact that you didn't need skilled men to build motor cars, so long as you gave them a repetitive job and standard components. Ford, after two earlier failures, brought out the fabulous Model T in 1908. It remained in production until 1927, when over 15 million vehicles had been sold. We all remember Ford, although some of us have forgotten the Oldsmobile.

All very interesting, these household names—Daimler, Benz, the four-stroke Otto cycle, tarmacadam—tarmac for short, diesel fuel, the Ford Foundation, Dunlop, the Michelin man: but you may wonder of what relevance they are in this context. The answer lies in Mr. Langdon's profession. Until motor vehicles were allowed to operate freely on public highways, virtually all movement of people or goods other than by rail or water involved horsepower. Every horse needed harness, and the harness was made and repaired by saddlers, as common in towns and villages as the smith, who made the farm implements and did the shoeing. Automation in American farming had been driven by a chronic labour shortage, leading to the development of everything from cotton gins to combine harvesters. In Europe labour remained plentiful and cheap, so

that more primitive agriculture, with its attendant tradesmen, survived. However, when
the motor vehicle replaced the horse and cart, the saddler's market shrank and his work
became scarce. Thomas Langdon was not alone among his trade in feeling the pinch.

In 1907 the first of the Langdon babies arrived, to be christened William. The
family moved to a house in Wiveliscombe High Street, where Mrs. Langdon was able
to keep 30 hens and continue with her egg business, encouraged by her husband
because the family needed the extra income. Thinking to expand her market beyond
Bristol, she spoke to a commercial traveller from London when he called at the
saddlery, suggesting that she might supply eggs for use in his firm's staff canteen. The
following week she received a draft contract stipulating that she would supply 40
dozen eggs a week from January to Easter, 1908. Thomas was against his wife's
signing a formal document of that type and for such an amount, especially outside the
main laying season. However, Mrs. Langdon signed, and proceeded to honour the
contract by scouring the district for supplies, although on occasion she had to make
a last-minute visit to her own hens to make up a deficit. The contract was not
renewed after Easter, when imported eggs became cheap and plentiful again, but a
point had been made. There was a market for west Somerset farm produce in
London, if producers were prepared to go and seek it out and use existing means of
transport for delivery.

Which came first, the chicken or the egg? In Mrs. Langdon's case, the egg, but in
1908 she decided to find out if she could replicate with chickens the marketing success
she was having with eggs. The problems were much the same. In the laying season
there was a glut of eggs in the countryside, and, to obtain a good price, they had to
be sold in the towns. If you kept chickens, you ended up with old birds and cockerels
beyond what could be eaten on the farm or sold profitably in the locality. There were
buyers, going from farm to farm to pick up unwanted birds, but paying wretched
prices. Maybe it would pay to explore the markets further afield.

And so, in 1908, on a visit to her husband's relatives in London, Mrs. Langdon
negotiated a contract with a chain of poultry and game shops which undertook to buy
good quality ready-dressed poultry from her by weight. Her existing egg suppliers were
only too pleased to have a similar outlet for their birds, at prices substantially better than
could be obtained on the farm. Every Thursday the dressed birds were collected or
delivered to Wiveliscombe, packed in the High Street premises and sent to London for
the weekend market. As the saddlery business continued to decline, Thomas Langdon
spent much of his time in a pony and trap collecting supplies from outlying farms. Four
children had now blessed their union, one of whom, as was so common in those days,
did not survive infancy. In addition to the family, Mrs. Langdon now had a full-time
job managing her business.

Before Christmas, or at any other time of special demand, Mrs. Langdon would
have a marquee erected in the garden, and friends and relations were pressed into
service to help pack the birds for dispatch. Another daughter arrived in 1912 without
affecting the progress of the business. Never mind the decline in saddlery. One trade
had replaced the other.

And then, in 1914, Armageddon. Shortly before war broke out, Thomas Langdon
sold the saddlery business and took over the *White Hart Hotel*, a traditional small town
inn in the centre of Wiveliscombe. Three-quarters of a century later the firm of
Langdons was to go back into the licensed trade, as we shall see in the fulness of time.

Without the railway, the efficient marketing of the country produce would not have been possible. The feeder services, to the premises in Wiveliscombe from the farms, and from the packing area to the station, were still operated by the traditional horse-drawn vehicles. Only one accident is recorded from those days. A cart with a load of eggs overturned in 1914, and the horse which was responsible was soon after called up for war service—or perhaps volunteered after seeing Kitchener's famous poster. That accident apart, things were going smoothly, and with the price of eggs up to 1s. 8d. a dozen for a hundred gross a week, and the poultry as well, it was turning into a very sweet little business.

Four

HOW THE GENERAL STRIKE AND THE GWR
LED MRS. LANGDON INTO TRANSPORT

After Thomas Langdon sold his saddlery business soon after the start of the First World War, he shared the running of the inn with his wife, who found herself rushed off her feet on market days, and drove a cart round the farms collecting produce. Two more children were to arrive. A son Philip, of whom more later, was born in 1918, and a daughter, Betty, in 1923.

Apart from the horse joining the forces, the first effect which the war had on the business was a dramatic increase in egg prices. These were later controlled to five shillings a dozen, which was 12 times as much as the young Bessie had had to accept 17 years earlier. Before the war, London egg prices had been kept low by Danish imports. With only domestic production available, the demand for Langdon eggs rose to 100 cases a week, and the higher price encouraged both farmers and cottagers to increase their flocks of laying hens. With more suppliers to visit and more produce to collect over a wider area, the Langdons found it difficult to get round the farms and make the station runs, relying as they did on horse-drawn carts. Although I doubt whether she ever knew or used the term, the reason why Mrs. Langdon succeeded in business was because she gave customer satisfaction. She appreciated that changes would be needed to provide better and more reliable methods of collection and concentration for the growing volume of goods if she were to hold her customers.

The chicken business carried on, and, with a wartime shortage of red meat, Mrs. Langdon started to trade in rabbits. From the days when they were introduced into the country by the Normans for food, rabbits had become a staple part of the diet in the countryside, although, given its noted fecundity, the species took a remarkable time to escape from its original burrows. Trappers, using ferrets, paid farmers for the right to take rabbits, the sum being agreed in advance on an estimate of the amount of the catch; the farmers were not prepared to go on what the trappers told them after the event, probably with good reason. The negotiation between farmer and trapper took the form of a joust in which each side obtained as much pleasure from doing down the other party as from making profit on the deal. However satisfactory that was to the contestants, it did not lead to a predictable and regular supply of rabbit meat for the London market.

Mrs. Langdon solved the problem by advancing cash to the trappers to buy, and pay in advance for, their franchises, taking her repayment in kind. By the end of the war she was sending over 1,500 rabbits a week to London in 40 cases, in addition to the poultry and those 100 cases of eggs, each case containing 30 dozen, or 36,000 eggs in total.

The business had been created because Mrs. Langdon worked out, or stumbled across, the simple verity that marketing, transport and distribution are as important in business as the initial production of the goods. Early in 1915, with the volume of produce continuing to grow, she replaced the ponies and traps with a Model T motor van. By then Henry Ford had been mass-producing these vehicles for seven years, which had been long enough to get most of the bugs out of them. The hilly country around Wiveliscombe was not best suited for a laden Model T, especially as the bottom gear ratio was on the high side. Happily the ratio in reverse was lower, and it was not uncommon to see a Ford being reversed up a steep hill.

It was suggested at the time that reversing the van was not one of Mrs. Langdon's stronger points. In those days there was no driving test, nor was there to be for many years after the Lords had suggested introducing one in 1924. Learners could therefore expect precious little instruction, which didn't matter too much as there wasn't a lot of traffic either, and what there was travelled comparatively slowly. Mrs. Langdon's first trip to the station to deliver eggs with the van resulted in a long detour as she was not at that time familiar with the operation of the reverse gear. I hope someone had told her how to double-declutch.

As the business grew, it became more difficult for Mrs. Langdon to juggle her time between the pub, the poultry and the children. The *White Hart* had its advantages, not least the skittle alley which doubled as a packing room. But with turkeys being added to the rabbits and the chickens, and the eggs, the time had come to give up inn-keeping and concentrate on the main chance. In 1917, therefore, the family moved to a large house in North Street, Wiveliscombe, which had the additional advantage of possessing a room which could be used as an office, with its own door to the street. There were still no employees in the business other than the family and casual helpers, but Mrs. Langdon needed somewhere to do her paperwork, other than on the kitchen table.

The war ended and prices fell to an extent that the poultry side of the business became barely profitable. The trade in rabbits did not drop away, and was to prosper until the early 1950s when myxomatosis ravaged the burrows and hedgerows. With local collection and shuttles to the station being made by truck, the Great Western Railway continued to enjoy a monopoly of the firm's deliveries, by now mainly to London. In 1919 the firm took on two employees who were not 'family' and in 1924 the eldest son, William, who had helped out since a child, went to Canada to make his fortune, deciding that there was not much prospect of doing well in British farming: perhaps also anxious to show that he could make his own way in life at a distance from his hard-working and hard-driving mother. Bill was to return in 1927, and play his part in the development of the business.

Then, in 1926 and 1927, two things happened which were eventually to lead to the business being divided between produce and distribution, although it was a long time before the separation finally came about. The first of these was the General Strike.

It is difficult for us, three quarters of a century later, to appreciate fully the impact the strike had on much of the population—on the middle classes certainly, but also on many labourers and trade unionists. The economic situation in the country, as in Europe, was unhealthy, the strength of sterling against the dollar encouraging imports and causing difficulties for exporters. By 1925, at \$4.86 to the £, the exchange rate had actually surpassed what it had been in 1914 when war had broken out. Contrary to colonialist mythology, the famed British Empire was in reality a financial burden on the Mother Country, only the Malay States, with their tin, rubber and copra, remitting back to the imperial treasury more than they cost militarily and administratively. The days of looting the Indians were long past.

Following a brief period of post-war prosperity while pent-up demand had been satisfied, many British manufactured goods had become uncompetitive. British coal, one of the staple industries employing directly over 300,000 men, the source of the famous 'black diamonds' on which the Industrial Revolution had fed, was suffering both from reduced demand and cheaper imports. Churchill's return to the Gold Standard in his 1925 Budget did nothing to ease the situation.

The year 1924 had seen damaging strikes. In January, the railwaymen were out for eight days, to be followed in February by the dockers. The Labour Prime Minister, Ramsay MacDonald, ruefully noted, 'The paradox of British politics: the moment one appropriates power one becomes impotent'. In October, he was voted out of office, but the industrial unrest continued. In 1925 the miners were bought off for a time by an agreement for a minimum wage, which, like all statutory minimum wages, is fine so long as the employers can afford to pay it, and for those who can find jobs. (These factors are not among those which politicians take into account when introducing acts of public benevolence at the expense of others. Statutory attempts to regulate wages and prices create distortions and shortages in the short term, and consequences the reverse of what was intended in the long term, the Rent and Mortgage Interest Protection Acts which were with us for more than sixty years proving the most salutary example.) In addition to the miners' minimum wage, a Royal Commission was established, with William Beveridge (later of Welfare State fame or notoriety) as one of its members, to make recommendations to resolve the dilemma facing the coal-mining industry. In the meanwhile a subsidy was paid to the collieries pending the completion of the Royal Commission's enquiry.

Peace was bought in this manner until March 1926, when the Commission presented its report. It recommended scrapping the minimum wage, ending the subsidy, and making wage cuts so that the 73 per cent of coal being mined at a loss could again be sold profitably. It also suggested the introduction of paid holidays and profit-sharing, which might have gone down better had there been more profits to share. The reaction of the miners was understandable and predictable. With the slogan 'Not a penny off the pay, not a minute off the day', they voted for a strike.

The industrial unrest was not the only circumstance which had been giving the general public cause for alarm. In the Zinoviev letter, now almost certainly exposed as a fake but only after the KGB secrets have been revealed, Soviet communists seemed to be giving their British counterparts instructions to start a revolution in these islands, to match their own against the Czar. It seemed to many that the Reds were not merely under the bed: they were trying to get between the sheets and commit rape. Meanwhile Hitler was emerging in Germany, although not yet seen as a threat, and Mussolini was already in power, encouraged no doubt by the Pope's assuring him that 'he had God's full protection'.

Against this background the miners started their strike on 1 May 1926. Two days later the TUC declared a General Strike in support. Apart from some rioting in Glasgow, the expected breakdown in society failed to materialise. The printers managed to stop the *Daily Mail* because they objected to an editorial, which gave Churchill the chance to bring out a pugnacious broadsheet. On the first day of the strike, only 849 trains ran, but within a week the figure was up to 5,500. Where lorry, bus and tram drivers came out, volunteers took over. A turning point was reached when armoured cars escorted 100 lorries laden with food into Hyde Park, to ensure that London did not starve.

With support crumbling and faced with wide public hostility, the TUC called off the General Strike on 12 May. But the harm had been done. Traders were no longer content to tolerate a situation where they could be pressurised, blackmailed as they might express it, by trade unionists pursuing a quarrel to which they were not a party. More damaging still, suppliers had learned that it was possible to move goods by road, as reliably and as cheaply as by rail.

The miners stayed out until 12 November, returning to work with their daily hours increased from seven to eight and faced with the introduction of divisive local wage bargaining. Other, longer-term, damage was done—the creation of that sense of martyrdom and resentment which enabled Arthur Scargill many years later to lead his troops into the hopeless battle against society in which the industry was finally brought low. Again it was the motor lorries, this time travelling in convoy with metal grilles protecting the glass in the cabs against missiles, which kept supplies moving, and helped the railway workers to drive yet another nail in their own coffin.

Mrs. Langdon was unable to deliver eggs to London by road during the General Strike. However, the Wiveliscombe brewers, Messrs Arnold and Hancock, kept production going by collecting raw materials by lorry from Avonmouth. They agreed to carry Langdon eggs to Bristol, if a Langdon employee would ride shotgun on their lorry to protect it against violence. There was no violence, and for the first time Langdon produce had successfully been transported from Wiveliscombe by road.

The General Strike proved, as strikes so often do, that there may well be a safer and better way of safeguarding the efficient running of a business than relying in future on those who had chosen, or been forced, to strike. For half a century, trade unionists and the general public considered another similar episode unthinkable, and gradually confidence in the unions, and appreciation for the protection they provided for employees, returned. Memories faded until the mould was again brutally shattered in the 1978-79 Winter of Discontent.

Apart from the single delivery to Bristol in May 1926, the Great Western Railway continued to enjoy Mrs. Langdon's business exclusively until 1927. There was, of course, no temperature-controlled road or rail transport in the 1920s, which meant that any delay in getting a perishable product like a dead rabbit or chicken to the customer was unwelcome and, in hot weather, potentially catastrophic. In the summer of 1927 several consignments of rabbits had arrived in London by rail smelling too high for culinary use. Then an important order of prime chickens was dispatched on the morning train for use in a City banquet. Leaving Wivesliscombe at 9.12, the consignment would have caught the 10.05 from Taunton and been in Paddington by 2.45 in the afternoon.

With kind permission of Mr. Colin Maggs.

Taunton Station *c.*1927 with the goods sidings full of wagons. The Rowbarton housing development built by Thomas Penny is top left.

Taunton goods station today.

The crate was marked 'To be called for at Paddington station' but in error was loaded on to a GWR delivery vehicle, along with other goods. The customer's van sent to collect the chickens returned from Paddington empty. Having made a long trip round London on a hot afternoon on the GWR vehicle, the birds were on arrival found not to be fit for the table.

In the transport and distribution business, these things happen, and if it is the fault of the haulier, and sometimes even if it isn't, the customer is only likely to be placated if someone quickly offers recompense, with a generous measure of humble pie thrown in. The modern Langdons does not go in for too many mission statements or similar gobbledegook but it has two company rules:

RULE 1 The Customer is always right.

RULE 2 If the Customer is wrong, see Rule 1.

(When recently a butter manufacturer with a split load, half for a British supermarket chain (with a short use-by date) and half for a customer in Central Europe (with a 90-day use-by date), neglected to identify which was which, both buyers rejected the goods, on the respective grounds that for an identical product the sell-by date was too long, or had already passed. Both refused to pay the manufacturer and Langdons had either to meet the loss or lose the account. Don't suggest please that at least they could get the butter back: just because a customer refuses to pay for goods on a technical point, that doesn't mean that they won't be sold.)

The Great Western Railway was not in the business of eating humble pie. It refused to pay for the unsaleable chickens, and the customer refused to order any more until Mrs. Langdon could guarantee efficient delivery. The General Strike had shown her what road transport could achieve. Against all advice, she decided to make future deliveries to London by road, and acquired a three-ton Chevrolet lorry. William 'Bill' Langdon, newly returned from Canada, became the first Langdons' long-distance lorry driver.

You may have noticed that little has been said about Thomas Langdon in our brief account of these turbulent years. While he had been landlord at the *White Hart*, he had never drunk alcohol, but after giving up the inn, he started drinking heavily and eventually became an alcoholic. Whether humilation at his own comparative failure and the success of his wife's business drove him to drink is a matter of pure speculation. His drinking, as always, led to much unhappiness in the family. In the end either his wife threw him out, as his grandson Peter suggests, or he decided to leave. He thereupon sold the family home, where he had been running a few head of cattle in a paddock, and moved to Bristol, where he died in 1935.

In those days, a breakdown in a marriage was rare; it was equally unusual for a woman to have a full-time job outside the home or to run a business; and exceptional for her to be the main bread-winner in the family. Perhaps what happened to the Langdons was no more than a precursor of what we now see in society generally, where by statute men and women share 'equal opportunities' and home-making is no longer regarded as a worthy occupation, except for a househusband. The unhappy years which Mrs. Langdon endured during the breakdown of her marriage must have been made more painful by the general knowledge in a small town of her husband's 'strong weakness', to use another delightful Irishism; and exacerbated by the prominence of her own position in that society. Today she would have had the consolation that separation and divorce no longer carry any social stigma, and nobody suffers, except the children of the marriage.

Five

HOW TAUNTON MOVED INTO THE MOTOR AGE AND MRS. LANGDON INTO GENERAL HAULAGE

On the rare occasions that I return to the place where I grew up, I am struck by how close the towns and villages have moved together in my absence. The reality is that I and my childhood friends revelled in the freedom that a bicycle gave young people in those days of light traffic. The towns and villages have not moved, but my changed method of transportation, to the motor car, has brought them closer.

The railways had the same effect on a society which had relied for transport on waterways, horses or its own feet. We have seen how a producer or dealer like Mrs. Langdon or the rectors of Heathfield could take advantage of access to markets which were formerly barred by remoteness. The effect on individuals, on passenger traffic, was less marked. The comparative infrequency of trains, coupled with the need for travellers to come and go at set times, and the cost, meant that social life still centred round the small town rather than gravitating towards the regional centre. Long after the advent of the motor age, Wiveliscombe and other Somerset towns and villages on the periphery of Taunton kept their courts and markets and shops and most of the trappings of a self-contained community. Wiveliscombe also had its celebrated brewery.

Yet year by year the pull of the county town, only 13 miles away, became stronger. Farmers started sending cattle to Taunton market where there more buyers and higher prices; housewives bought excursion tickets to go shopping in Taunton; and those in business began to see Taunton as a more convenient place in which to locate because of its better communications and the urban amenities. All Mrs. Langdon's shipments went east through the county town and she had now reached the limit of the eggs she could collect in the Wiveliscombe area. If the business of Langdons was to grow, she had better start thinking about moving out of Wiveliscombe and broadening the firm's base. (We will abandon the apostrophe in Langdon's from henceforward, except when used as a possessive adjective (Langdons'), although 'Chambers's' was still 'Chambers's' a century later.)

Mrs. Langdon's first move was in the Taunton direction, but only as far as the next village down the line, to Milverton. That was in 1927. By 1930 she had taken over a Taunton business as well, as will be revealed shortly. Then, as we will see, in 1935, she acquired another business in Taunton.

Our last look at Taunton was through the eyes of the anonymous contributor to *Chambers's Encyclopaedia* in 1874. We have already noted some of the effects which the development of transportation in west Somerset was having on rural communities. Let us pause for a page or two to consider how the same phenomenon, the shrinking of distance, was shaping the evolution of its principal town.

As you might expect, by the 20th century, the west Somerset canals were in effect finished. In the 1930s, the Bridgwater and Taunton carried very little traffic other than wood for the timber merchants, Pennys. The last barge carrying coal for Goodlands, the coal merchants, docked in Taunton in 1907. The Bristol and Exeter Railway Company had acquired the other canal serving the town, the Great Western leading to Tiverton, in 1867. The railway company had almost at once closed the stretch between Taunton and Loudwells, and the land adjoining Taunton station had been incorporated in the marshalling yards for goods wagons. Surprisingly, traffic on the other end of the canal lingered on until 1924, with William Elworthy, who owned Whipcott Quarry, moving 7,000 tons of stone weekly by barge into Tiverton for crushing.

The Devon market town Barnstaple, at the other end of the railway which passed through Norton Fitzwarren and Wiveliscombe, boasted three railway stations: four if you included the separate platform at Barnstaple Town for the narrow-gauge Lynton and Barnstaple Railway during its troubled life between 1898 and 1923, and five if you counted their halt at Barnstaple Yard. Taunton, much larger than Barnstaple, had only one, the size and financial muscle of the Great Western Railway having kept out predators. As was often the case, Taunton station had been built some distance from the town centre, where land was cheaper and more freely available. As traffic grew, there were reconstructions and additions, of which the most significant relating to the station itself took place in 1895 and 1900. Warehouses for storage and consolidation of goods in the entrepôt trade were constantly extended. The metals were quadrupled towards Bristol and towards Exeter, giving four tracks in place of two, and an aerial photograph taken in the 1920s shows the thriving state of the goods traffic, with some 150 wagons in the sidings.

One of the more bizarre investments the Great Western made was as late as 1937 when the track was doubled from Norton Fitzwarren to Milverton, the station before Wiveliscombe. But the GWR never looked on this line as a branch despite its moorland meanderings, giving it equal cartographical status in its timetables with the route between Paddington and Plymouth.

If you need more evidence of the omnipotence and reach of the railways, you need only recall that the coverage of the country which they provided at the turn of the century was such that, until its railway to Barnstaple opened, Lynton was the largest community in England not to be connected to the system. And Lynton was, and is, a pretty small place.

In August 1901 the distance of the station from the town centre brought another Taunton railway enterprise into being: well, not exactly a railway, but a tramway which ran from East Reach to the station under the grandiloquent style of The Taunton and West Somerset Electric Railways and Tramways Company Limited. Wherever stations were built away from a town centre, the town was almost certain to develop in that direction. That happened in Taunton too. Thomas Penny, who still brought his timber to his yard by barge, carried the process even further by building a large housing estate beyond the station in the district of Rowbarton, and the trams followed him there in August 1909.

In 1921 the Borough Councillors, who owned the municipal Electricity Company, wanted to charge the tram company an economic rate for its power, which was unfortunately more than that fragile concern could afford to pay. It thereupon went out of business, being only the second tram operator in the country to fail. Its garages were to be brought into profitable use later, as will be revealed in due course. In those days there was no taxation without representation, with businesses having votes in local elections as well as householders: but also no representation without taxation. This meant that the money councillors chose to spend came out of their own pockets and businesses, and those of their constituents, rather than mainly through subventions from central funds as today: and there was no point in squandering it in an effort to

North Street, Taunton c.1906 with a car, a tram, and a cart lettered G.W.R.

buy votes. Furthermore, most councillors were in commerce themselves and accustomed to the careful handling of money. We all know what ensues when the connection between the raising and spending of public funds is broken, and when those with no business experience find themselves in a position to spend large sums of other people's money and show what public benefactors they are.

(I had an interesting glimpse of the changed world of municipal finance in the 1960s. The Taunton Borough Surveyor was a Mr. Tyzack who unfortunately underestimated the cost of sewage works at Ham downstream from the town by what was then a significant sum of around £50,000. Fearing difficulties in Council, he put on the agenda an item raising the question of what contribution staff should make towards their ball-point pens, costing around one shilling each, but partly used for private purposes. The last item on the agenda was approval for the cost excess at Ham. The Councillors spent over twenty minutes on the pen issue, and two minutes approving the £50,000. As he explained to me at the time, 'You see, they understand a shilling, but not fifty thousand'.)

The first motor car recorded in Taunton was in 1897, and within a few years complaints were being made about the nuisance being caused by motor traffic in the town. Although motor taxis appeared in 1907, the Council decided the following year to renew its horse-drawn fire engine with a similar device, perhaps preferring reliability to rapidity, only changing their collective minds in favour of the internal combustion engine, and speedier response, in 1924. The Great Western also relied on horses for onward delivery and a photograph of the period shows a tram passing through what to us would seem a deserted street, with a horse-drawn GWR delivery cart in the foreground.

Taunton businesses and shops between the wars, and for some time after 1950, remained in the hands of local families, the proprietor working in a firm which had his surname above the door. Thus in the three department stores, you would find Mr. Hatcher at Hatchers, Mr. Chapman at Chapmans, and Messrs Clements and Brown at Clements and Brown. Alderman Goodland ran the coalyard, and the Council, and the Bench, assisted by Alderman William Penny, who imported the wood and sat on the Bench and in the Council. Alderman van Trump, who served as Mayor for four years, established a clothing firm which bore his name, having started his business career as a pawnbroker. Only James Pearsall, the silk throwsters who had been in the town since the 18th century, had no Pearsall on its letterhead. The three local bankers, Fox's, Stuckeys and Badcocks, were the first locally-owned businesses to sell out to the national multiple organisations, Lloyds and the Westminster gaining the best prizes. (A story, perhaps apocryphal, was told of a message sent by a Wellington director in the old days before a Board meeting in telegraphese: *CAN'T COME BAD COLD BADCOCK*. A viral, not a venereal, indisposition was indicated.)

After the First World War Taunton, despite its superb rail links with the rest of the country and the county, found its growth and prosperity being curtailed by congestion at the single bridge over the river Tone between the station and the town centre. A second bridge was built in 1921 for £12,000 within a couple of hundred yards of the goods yard, which had the effect of strengthening the railway's grip on the carriage of merchandise. The cattle market was also moved from the Parade in the centre of the town to a site adjacent to the new bridge and the railway.

Throughout the 1920s and 1930s, the railway sheds and platforms were crowded with goods for outward dispatch by rail or final inbound delivery by road, including supplies for most of the shops. For all its size, the GWR was managed for the benefit of its shareholders and customers as well as its staff. Beside the station, the *Great Western Hotel* was provided for the convenience of travellers, not turned into offices for bureaucrats as was to happen soon after nationalisation. But the writing was on the wall, for those who chose to read it, as lorries, both steam and petrol driven, increasingly made their ominous appearance in the streets.

Which takes us back to 1927 and the Chevrolet three-tonner which Bill Langdon, with a co-driver, drove to London at least three times a week, and five if trade was brisk. Keeping to the timetable established by dispatch by rail, the lorry left Wivelisscombe at around 6 p.m. and arrived back next morning at around 9.00, after which it would be used by another driver for local collection during the day. This established the pattern of what is known as trunking in the modern transport business, whereby two drivers working shifts are able to make more intensive use of one truck, although they drive alone and neither has a mate in the cab with him—or if he does, it is not connected with the operation of the vehicle. Langdons did not refine the system by using the vehicle on its return leg for traffic destined for the West Country until 1933.

The first time the Langdons' lorry was used to carry goods for third parties was in the winter of 1930, when farmers in the Brendons were cut off from normal supplies through heavy snow. It was, however, difficult to exploit the potential for return loads without somewhere to break bulk. The ideal world in which traffic from A to B is perfectly matched by traffic from B to A does not exist. The best you can hope for is a full load outward bound, and bits and pieces which make up part of a load for part of the way on the return journey. If the vehicle is carrying a single product on its return journey, that will almost certainly be something which is destined to be shared among several users. To secure return loads on a regular basis, you need a warehouse at your home base which can be devoted to sorting and dispatching inward traffic, and then a means of economically delivering it to each final destination. The railway had such a strong grip on the carriage of goods and was such a formidable competitor, because it had established this entrepôt structure country-wide: my family firm, which manufactured clothing in Essex, was still sending all its output by rail, and in particular to Hatchers and Chapmans in Taunton, until well after the Second World War. (It did not help customer confidence in the LNER's services when their compensation for damage and theft each month usually exceeded the freight bill. A bigger problem resulted from the loss of clothing coupons, which the railway was unable to replace.)

Every cloud, so they say, has a silver lining. When Mrs. Langdon parted from her husband Thomas and he sold the property in North Street, Wiveliscombe, she bought for herself and the children a house in Church Street, with plenty of ground in its curtilage for putting up a garage and a warehouse. The Chevrolet on its journey home was thus able to collect pig and poultry feed from mills at Avonmouth destined for west Somerset, of which the bulk would be broken in Wiveliscombe, and the individual orders delivered to the farms in the same vehicle as was collecting dairy produce and eggs for up-country.

With her contacts among the farmers and in the cities, it was natural that Mrs. Langdon should start dealing in other dairy products such as cheese and butter in addition to the chickens, eggs and rabbits. She had learned the hard way that you lose customers if you don't control the quality of the product you are selling. City liverymen won't eat stinking chickens nor game merchants buy rotten rabbits. The product not only has to leave the producer in good condition: it also has to arrive in good condition.

Initially she had problems with the farm butter, because the flavour would vary according to the milk used from different herds. She was able to provide a consistent quality and taste by mixing the output of various farms until she had a standard product, which was then weighed and wrapped by hand. As we will see shortly, she was also to become an important player in the task of ensuring egg quality on a national basis.

There were now, as we move into the 1930s, three vans to cover the work of the old Model T, doing the local collection and delivery, sometimes assisted by the lorry: but only the one lorry still. A photograph of the firm's stand at the Bath and West Show in 1936 shows two men and a woman engaged at a packing machine, the name of the firm being strangely absent. Perhaps everyone knew by then that eggs meant Langdons. It was certainly beginning to look that way.

Six

HOW MRS. LANGDON AT LANGDONS AND MR. ROWLEY AT TAUNTON CIDER SURVIVED BETWEEN THE WARS

One of the consequences of a major war is that a surviving combatant may have learned a deadly trade and gained valuable experience in its practice, but finds himself unequipped to make a comparable living in peacetime, except as a mercenary, and that usually turns out to be not much of a career either. Many of the men who were demobilised in Britain after the Second World War had been called up fresh from school and had for years been flying aeroplanes, captaining ships, leading assaults up defended beaches and so on, and when peace came were still barely out of their teens. Those whose education had been interrupted by war service and found themselves without a trade or profession received generous help from the state, along with their demob suit, when they returned to civilian life: but, thankfully, no counselling.

The survivors of the First World War were less fortunate. Clinging to their dignity and wartime ranks, and having often experienced horrors more intense and prolonged than those met by combatants in the Second War, they frequently sought to make their way in businesses for which they had neither the capital nor the expertise. Two of my uncles found themselves in this unhappy plight between the wars, and for one of them the award of the highest decoration for bravery delivered no more than the post of assistant manager at a provincial hotel, from which he only managed to escape on being appointed a Colonel in the Home Guard.

Such too was the lot of Captains Bennett and Gamlin, who used their meagre gratuities on demobilisation in 1919 to set themselves up as egg merchants in Milverton, bordering on Mrs. Langdon's territory. Like her they bought a collection van. They also tried to turn to their advantage the laying season, when eggs were cheaper, by acquiring large tanks which they filled with waterglass, a solution of sodium silicate in which it was common to preserve eggs for later use both in the home and in industry. The plan came unstuck because of those same imported eggs which had brought to an end Mrs. Langdon's first London contract way back in 1908. The gallant pair would have been better advised to have installed a battery for hens of their own, as their competitor next down the line was to do in 1928.

Mrs. Langdon bought their van and other assets in 1927, without paying anything for the goodwill. This addition of the Milverton collection round, coupled with the elimination of competition, increased her hold on egg production over a wide area. She thus found herself well-placed after 1929 to pick off any weak competitor, when economic disasters world-wide dried up credit and the world found itself in the Great Depression.

The economic situation might have been handled better had there been a federal Central Bank, a 'Fed', in the United States. That function was performed, if at all, on an *ad hoc* basis by the great financial house of J.P. Morgan. The New York and other American stock exchanges had seen spectacular rises in share prices, encouraging many who could not afford the risk to speculate on margin, on the basis that prices could only go up, and make their fortunes. At 11.30 a.m. eastern time on 24 October 1929 the bubble burst. After a morning of frantic selling and prices which found no floor,

Thomas W. Lamont, the senior partner of J.P. Morgan, told the world that there had been a little distress selling, technical rather than fundamental. He was wrong. That afternoon 11 investors committed suicide. The Great Depression had started.

Today such a failure in the American economy would instantly involve the rest of the world, and especially industrialised nations. Seven decades ago, the ripples spread just as surely but more slowly. Unemployment grew in the United Kingdom, reaching 1.5 million in March 1930 and continued rising. In August, the figure had risen to 2,011,467, of whom three quarters were male. The Labour minister, Sir Oswald Mosley, advocated massive spending on public works to create work and avoid depression. When his remedies were rejected, he resigned from the government and his place as Chancellor of the Duchy of Lancaster was taken over by Clement Attlee. On 22 July, the German mark became worthless. On 24 August, an all-party Government of National Unity took over from Labour after the governor of the Bank of England, Sir Montagu Norman, had warned that the country faced bankruptcy. On 20 September, Britain left the Gold Standard and the £ was devalued by 30 per cent, from 4.86 to 3.40 against the dollar.

Slowly confidence was restored, but only after numerous business failures, and great distress among those without work, and their families. Everywhere pay was being reduced, and when a cut was imposed on naval ratings, 12,000 of them mutinied. There were violent clashes between unemployed rioters and the police in London, Bristol and other cities. Mosley established his British Union of Fascists, to emulate the apparent order and progress of Mussolini's Italy, of which the only positive thing most people could find to say was that the trains ran on time. Hitler came to power in Germany. On 8 October 1932, Governor Roosevelt of New York was elected President of the United States, winning 42 of the 49 states, and in June 1933 he announced his New Deal, which despite, or perhaps because of, the remedies being similar to those adopted by Mussolini in Italy and advocated by Mosley, triggered the recovery which continued until the outbreak of the Second World War. He also repealed Prohibition, and not before time. It had already led to a general acceptance of law-breaking, which in turn led to a change in the nature of crime exemplified by the Mafia. This damage to society is inevitable if any law is passed with which the majority of the population disagree and which they are prepared to flout. The legacy of Prohibition, and the disrespect for law which it engendered, haunt the United States to this day.

This potted reminder of a desperate era introduces us to another group of ex-army officers who, beguiled by the immediate post-war price of eggs, had sunk their gratuities into chicken farms. They had also formed a co-operative under the style of Taunton Vale Egg Producers to run a communal egg-packing station employing two girls in Taunton and operating under a voluntary code of quality known as the National Mark Scheme. This quality certification had been established as a supposed guarantee of the superior properties of British eggs, which would thereby command a higher price than imports. Mrs. Langdon had long operated her own strict control on the grading and condition of eggs, as with rabbits, chickens and so on. Because the National Mark Scheme was voluntary and not at first properly monitored by independent inspectors, she was convinced it would not prevent poor quality eggs reaching the market, and so damage all British producers in the eyes of the public, as indeed happened.

Late in 1929 the ex-officers who owned the grandiloquently named Taunton Vale Egg Producers, finding themselves like so many others in financial difficulties, appealed to Mrs. Langdon to help them. After a prudent delay for thought and negotiation, she took over the egg-packing business, transferred the two girls to Wiveliscombe, and agreed to handle the officers' eggs for them in future at twopence a dozen, or only twice what the young Bessie had been charging her neighbours in the 1890s. The deal was represented at the time, and by her biographer, as an act of benevolence; but it was also good business.

A great many firms survived the depression even though they operated at a loss in the years from 1930 to 1935, and the Somerset Egg & Poultry Company in Taunton was one of them. Despite its modern premises and an impressive list of customers which included providing eggs for the Atlantic liners based in Southampton, its owners, Bristol Industries Ltd, were unable to make it pay. They put it on the market, with its sheds for fattening 5,000 head of poultry, its egg-packing facilities and its cold store. After a long haggle, Mrs. Langdon bought the stock and equipment at valuation, and leased the premises from the vendor. Wisely she looked at the business for six months after the purchase without altering much and, when it continued to lose money, she introduced as manager her first non-family employee who had joined the firm in 1919, Arthur Bristow.

With Mr. Bristow in charge, it was easy to introduce the working practices which made the parallel Wiveliscombe operation profitable. She gained further economies by co-ordinating the onward transport arrangements of the two locations. The Taunton collections were covered by three vans, as were those from Wiveliscombe. The trunking pattern was varied to enable the reliable Chevrolet to cover the great Hampshire ports of Southampton and Portsmouth as well as London. Only one weekly run was direct to London. The other three journeys there involved part loads for either of the ports. This introduction of intermediate 'drops' inaugurated another stage in the development of the transport side of Langdons. Bill Langdon was also introduced to an industrial world far removed from the easy-going fellowship of west Somerset. One of his first loads for Southampton consisted of eggs for the maiden voyage of the *Queen Mary*, in 1935. He duly parked where he was told and unloaded his eggs, with a lot of sullen observers standing idly by. When he had completed the job, a supervisor appeared from the dock office and told him to reload them on the lorry. Unloading was dockers' work.

Using her own vehicles for collection and delivery seems pretty mundane to us these days but, at the time, what Mrs. Langdon was doing, with Bill's help, was unusual. Most traders with goods to deliver used the railway because it was reliable, quick, reasonably efficient, regular, had a standard tariff and above all offered comprehensive coverage of the whole country. Cost and competitiveness were not a major factor as, with its market dominance, the railway set the rate for all, the price which others had to meet. The great disadvantage it suffered against road transport was the need to trans-ship the goods at least twice, and often much more, or what is now known as 'cross-docking'. Each time goods have to be moved from a vehicle into a warehouse, into a warehouse from a vehicle, from a train to a platform, from a platform to another train, it costs money and there is a risk of damage, theft or human error. Direct shipment by road eliminated these hazards. A lorry could pick up a load at a warehouse, and deliver it to its eventual customer without intermediate handling or picking. ('Picking' is the process of selecting goods in a warehouse from bulk and dispatching them to various destinations.)

There were several reasons why road transport, with such an apparent advantage over rail, failed for so long to attract more of the nation's transport business. For a start, the carrying capacity of lorries was tiny both in terms of weight and bulk. The famous Chevrolet was a three-tonner as compared with a modern articulated tractor and trailer which have a permitted gross weight under normal operation of 41 tonnes and, if travelling to a railhead, 44 tonnes. Weight and volume were never a problem for trains. Furthermore, in the 1930s, lorries were temperamental, and the tyres especially were liable to punctures

Taunton Cider Ltd between the Wars.

and bursts. Repair facilities were available only in the larger towns, and there was no national recovery service for lorries. The roads were poor, without dual carriageways or overtaking facilities, passing through the centre of each town and village on the way. Before 1939, only Kingston, on the A30 to the south-west, was to have its famous bypass, with its novel underpasses and separate double lanes in each direction.

To justify sending goods by road, a full load was needed, at least on the outward journey, and preferably some revenue on the return. In effect, to make its own long-distance deliveries by road, a firm needed to turn itself also into a transport company. Mrs. Langdon's achievement, or one of them, was that she did precisely that.

Eggs, dairy products and poultry, however, remained her main interest. Between 1935 and 1938 she established another line by taking surplus milk from the farms and supplying bottled cream for the London market. This business was killed when lorries started collecting milk churns daily from the farms, establishing for the first time the mystique of the 'milk cheque' which has sustained dairy farmers to this day.

In 1937 Langdons was finding difficulty in ensuring regular and sufficient supplies of eggs and chickens from farmers to satisfy its growing markets, despite the acquisition of the businesses in Milverton and Taunton and the setting-up of the battery for 400 laying birds in Wiveliscombe. In 1937 therefore Mrs. Langdon bought a 38-acre poultry farm with 4,000 laying birds at Bindon in Somerset, which son Bill Langdon managed, in addition to his other work. The pundits call this vertical integration.

At the outbreak of war in September 1939, Langdons was part-producing and processing 25 tons of eggs a week, and sending to London 2,000 rabbits and 1,000 birds prepared for the table. It had twin bases in Wiveliscombe and Taunton, used six vans and the lorry, and employed 25 people, including sons Bill and Philip, and daughter Betty. Mrs. Langdon's personal status in the industry had been recognised when, in 1936, she was appointed a director of the company responsible for running the national egg quality scheme. She had also become, by all accounts, a wealthy woman, much respected or envied in the community, and a member of the Rural District Council.

While Mrs. Langdon had been prospering, Frank Rowley had made slow progress in widening the market for the products of the Taunton Cider Company Limited, of which he remained an active, but non-executive, Chairman, with George Pallett still running the firm in Norton Fitzwarren. The '20s and '30s seem to have been relatively unexciting times at Norton Fitzwarren, with Taunton Cider not much different from a host of other small producers. The business produced mainly draught cider, which was the less profitable or commodity end of the trade. In the late 1920s Rowley, through his London connections, developed some outlets in the free licensed trade of the Home Counties. Because these customers needed bottled cider, the firm established a bottling plant in London, the scale of which can be inferred from its location under the railway arches in South Harrow. Even this modest expansion was unable to survive the depression, and the railway arches were vacated in 1934.

Mr. Rowley brought off a more successful and significant piece of business in 1927 following a serious fire at the Oakhill Brewery, near Bath, which brought to an end its cider production because the remaining resources were needed for brewing beer. He persuaded Oakhill to supply its tied houses with Taunton Cider which he sold them at a shilling a gallon and, to cement the contract, persuaded them to take up 6 per cent of the equity in Taunton Cider, with the power to nominate a director to the Taunton board. When Oakhill later expanded in mergers with the Charlton Brewery and Bristol United Breweries, Taunton Cider was sold through their tied houses also.

Other than to Oakhill, the main sales outlet during these pre-war years was through the person of one Alfred Jeanes, whom Taunton Cider appointed as its agent in 1933, paying him £10 a month, with 5 per cent on all the sales he made. Jeanes had been an independent cider maker and pea grower from North Petherton, which lies between Taunton and Bridgwater. His business had failed in 1930. Happily he proved better at selling cider than he had been in the pea business, and he was to remain in effect Taunton Cider's sole commercial traveller until he was asked to retire in 1950, his health failing through his having sampled the wares which he was peddling rather too assiduously for the good of his liver. The story that he simultaneously represented Sheppeys, another local cider maker, is probably untrue. When, however, he was dismissed by Taunton Cider, he approached a French cider maker for a job, and worked for them for a while.

By 1939, Jeanes was supplying 350 public houses. He even sold cider from a stall on market days. He liked the trade so much that he took the *Victoria Inn* in Taunton for his wife to run, while he pursued his cider business.

In their different ways, the Oakhill deal and Jeanes's calling on customers were precursors of a style of marketing that was to make Taunton Cider a household name and bring substantial employment and prosperity to Norton Fitzwarren. The tie-up with Oakhill showed the advantage of having guaranteed demand through tied houses, and was to influence the thinking of the Taunton Cider management in the post-war years. The contract with Alfred Jeanes showed that constant calling on publicans led to increased business.

Then war broke out. On 31 May 1940 Oswald Mosley was interned along with two members of parliament, one Labour and one Conservative, and 33 of his followers. Family gossip has it that one of my other uncles in Scotland came close to joining him in Brixton prison. Attlee, Mosley's successor in office, became Deputy Prime Minister. It is chastening to contemplate that, but for his resignation from the Labour Party a decade earlier, Oswald Mosley might have been Winston Churchill's deputy in the fight against Hitler.

Seven

How Langdons and Taunton Cider Came Through the Second World War

It is a measure of Britain's preparedness for war that one of the first acts taken by the government in the defence of the realm in September 1939 was to treat the trusty Langdons' Chevrolet in the way the unfortunate horse had been treated in 1914: it was requisitioned, along with three of the vans. They perhaps made their contribution to the defeat of Hitler other than by being parked in a guarded compound until the tyres rotted, the bodies rusted and the engines fell out, although I wouldn't like to wager on it. It is doubtful if any of the vehicles was fit or youthful enough to see service with the British Expeditionary Force in France. Mrs. Langdon's younger son, Philip, in the firm since leaving school, had joined the Territorial Army and was called up immediately. Bill Langdon was later to join the Royal Air Force. In all 20 men from the firm served in the war. The departure of able-bodied men from small businesses did not happen overnight, but by 1941 all of them had gone. Any adult male able to breathe and walk had no difficulty in passing the stringent standards set by the medical examiners: outside a reserved occupation, only flat feet could keep a man under 40 out of the services. That left Mrs. Langdon and her teenage daughter Betty to run the business.

Two of the most successful television programmes of recent years have been *Yes, Minister* and *Dad's Army*. They succeeded because, like all good comedy and satire, they do not stray far from reality. Those of us, whose good fortune it has been to work in or with public bodies and to observe at first hand the ambition, guile, intelligence, charm, inexperience and vanity of Permanent Under-Secretaries and Ministers of the Crown, relish their accurate portrayal and caricature in the characters of Jim Hacker, Sir Humphrey Appleby and the superb Secretary to the Cabinet, Arnold.

So too with the world of Warmington-on-Sea. My own Home Guard commander, a Barclays Bank manager, were he alive today would surely be drawing royalties for each repeat programme, so blatant is Captain Mainwaring's plagiarism. The series also reminds those who lived through those days of the shortages, and the spivs who developed the black market: the patriotism and sacrifice, but also the selfishness: the dangers of bombing, and the speed with which civilians became accustomed to it: and a new feature in British life, the tyranny of officialdom, exemplified in *Dad's Army* by Air Raid Warden Hodges.

A reason why Britain remains an uneasy member of a European Community whose laws are made in Brussels and adjudicated upon in Strasbourg is that there is a different mindset between a society operating under English Common Law, and one which uses the Code Napoleon, Roman Law, and their derivatives. Under Common Law, the individual citizen is allowed to do anything which is not expressly declared illegal. This gives wide personal freedom, coupled with a responsibility not to abuse that freedom. It is noteworthy that, almost without exception, the scandals which have rocked the City of London, from Cedar Holdings to Guinness and Maxwell, have involved people whose family upbringing had not inculcated in them an understanding of the implicit contract between the individual and society upon which English Common Law is based.

Taunton Cider employees clocking off between the wars.

Those nurtured under the continental system play by different rules. There, stupid or oppressive laws are not strictly enforced and the state, through its officials, operates a system for which the French word *tolérance* equates more with the engineering tolerance, the degree of permitted error in a manufactured part which will enable the whole to function, than with the general meaning, a willingness to accept differences. In the same sense in those societies, if the application of a law means that the country may suffer harm, then the law must be circumvented. To protect French industry, for example, it is quite permissible to keep a British product out of the market by the use of non-tariff barriers, whatever the law says. Thus in the transport industry French trailers built to inferior standards are freely available on the British market, while the superior equipment manufactured by Gray and Adams Ltd in Fraserburgh is kept out of France by the usual accumulation of non-tariff barriers of which British Eurocrats, almost invariably seduced by the trappings of power in Brussels, remain unaware, however slowly and carefully you explain the process to them and however much evidence is laid before them.

(Anticipating our story by half a century, it is worth mentioning that Langdons were to develop a close and fruitful relationship with Gray and Adams, and I was fortunate enough to become a personal friend of its Chairman Jim Gray, in part through a bizarre coincidence. In 1993 I helped an Irish business with a management buy-out and, when it established a Scottish company in Fraserburgh, I acted for a while as its Chairman. The Scottish business prospered in a shed which adjoined the Gray and Adams factory and soon ran out of space for expansion. Although a site on which to build a bigger factory was available in the town, bureaucratic obstructionism and delay prevented progress until Jim Gray had words in the right quarter.)

In September 1939 the expected hail of German bombs did not fall. The cardboard coffins stored in the mortuaries and the lime-pits which had been dug to act as mass graves for the 100,000 casualties expected in the first few weeks lay empty. Instead the public were bombarded with a welter of government regulations designed to control all aspects of private and business life. In every community patriotic citizens were to be found, wearing first makeshift armbands, and then uniforms, determined that each of these rules and regulations should be observed, to the letter, whether relevant to national security and welfare or not, with all the rigour that applied to statutory offences. The cry 'Put that Light Out' was heard every evening across the land.

Animal feeds were among the first products to be controlled. The Ministry took over all supply. Bulk distribution from Avonmouth to Wiveliscombe, and onward to the farms, stopped. With her remaining vans, Mrs. Langdon contrived to maintain outward deliveries to London by road until 1940, but the development of the transport business in parallel with the eggs and chickens came to a halt. The shortage of feeding stuffs also made it impossible to continue raising birds for the table and those operations were closed down. In 1941 the Ministry of Food introduced zoning, allocating to each egg-packing station an area in which it was permitted to collect eggs. Langdons were designated the collector for Taunton, Wellington, Wiveliscombe, half of Bridgwater and the country in-between. Prices were fixed and firms were given an allocation out of which to supply the population in their allotted area, any surplus being handed over to the Ministry. All scope for enterprise or initiative vanished and, in any event, profits in excess of those made pre-war were taxed at 100 per cent.

Food rationing was introduced on 8 January 1940, starting with butter, sugar, bacon and ham. Meat rationing followed the next month, although rabbits remained off the ration. The legacy of the Normans, the conquerors who introduced rabbits for food, was about to come into its own. As we have seen, Mrs. Langdon had the contacts among the trappers, and was able from 1940 to send not less than 2,000 rabbits a week to market, although they had to be sold at controlled prices. A demand was also developing for rooks, and rook pie found its way back to a few urban dinner tables.

Betty Langdon worked throughout the war as cashier, van driver and general factotum. She was fortunate to be still a teenager in December 1941 when, faced with no reserves of manpower, the government introduced conscription for all women, married or single, between the ages of 20 and 40. By then all boys had had to register for call-up and join the Home Guard or undergo some other kind of military training at 16, entering the services at 18 years and six months. At the other end of the scale, men up to 50 also became liable for military service, although in practice, unlike what you see in the war films, few of those older than 25 had the stamina to cope with the privations and demands of active service.

The war ended in September 1945. Bill and Philip Langdon were demobilised, along with other staff. The only relics of the war that remained undamaged were the regulations, controls, restrictions and quotas which the socialist government under Attlee saw no reason for abolishing, the omnipresent officials who had grown use to the exercise of arbitrary, if often futile, power, and the desperate shortages of food, fuel and consumer goods.

Almost alone among west-country towns, Taunton escaped the war with virtually no bomb damage and it was left to the councillors and planners, rather than Hitler, to oversee the demolition and replacement of many of the individual buildings which had been an attractive feature of its streets and squares. Fortunately other old buildings remain and are perhaps more cherished than they once were. The American army had built a huge military hospital in Musgrove Park, on the edge of town, which remained behind them to supplement, and then replace, a Victorian building in East Street, with its Conservators Ward a reminder that navigation on the river Tone had once proved a profitable business. In Norton Fitzwarren a large Supply Reserve Depot (SRD) had been built during the war for the army, complete with rail sidings and numerous warehouses. This will feature again in our story and it too might, like the hospital, have been almost a gift to the community but for the dogmatism of a Chairman of the Finance Committee of the Somerset County Council.

(Some twenty years later, in the mid-1960s, the SRD was released by the army and offered for sale at a figure slightly below £500,000. It transpired that the local authority would have priority in buying the property at what was a knock-down price. This would have secured for Taunton an industrial estate and a location for building 'starter units' for small tradesmen. The Taunton optical manufacturer Avimo had been obliged to build, and then expand, a factory in Barnstaple because of the unavailability of a site in Taunton. The County Planning Officer, Mr. Dale, was keen that the County Council should buy the property and relieve the pressure on industrial land and buildings. The Chairman of the County Council Finance Committee said the purchase could not be made as no funds were available. The pay-back period at the asking price was just under two years. I happened to be meeting in London every week the Permanent Under-Secretary of the Ministry of Housing and Local Government, (then Mr.) I.V. Pugh, who was an assessor of a Committee of which I was a member. He at once agreed to grant the County Council an appropriate loan. Dale was delighted but the Chairman on the County Council Finance Committee remained obdurate, refusing even to take the matter before the full Council. The site was later sold commercially.)

When the war ended, with the shopping centres of Bath, Bristol, Yeovil, Exeter and Plymouth in ruins, Taunton found itself for a few years the only major town in the west country which had emerged with its retail facilities intact. In the immediate post-war period, and indeed for years afterwards, clothing and furniture were rationed as well as food, but in Taunton at least there were shops in which traders could display what was available.

Another legacy of the war was the engineering plant, Avimo Ltd, which had been established in 1936 by a French manufacturer who feared that war with Germany was coming, and wanted a safer haven for his money and himself when it did, as he had been convinced that France would fall to the Germans. Unlike many firms which grew in wartime making military products, Avimo managed to diversify its manufacture, widen its markets and develop its own products. It remains a significant employer in the town. In the following years, the shirt and clothing manufacturers, which included some which had been household names, went bankrupt or closed one by one in the face of rising labour costs and cheap foreign imports.

We left Taunton Cider when the war began, still producing cider in Norton Fitzwarren and selling it mainly through the Oakhill Brewery's outlets and through the agency of the indefatigable Alfred Jeanes. Langdons and Taunton Cider were about the same size in 1939 but the zoning which reduced Langdons to egg-packers and rabbit merchants in a restricted area worked in Taunton Cider's favour when the company was awarded a distribution zone which included the public houses of the dominant local brewer, Starkey, Knight and Ford. Starkey's owned its own cider factory, the Quantock Vale Cider Company, which, like Taunton Cider, employed some 15 people. When the output from Quantock Vale proved insufficient to satisfy the wartime demand in Starkey houses, Taunton Cider was designated as the supplier to make up the deficit. It was not a question of having to make a sale. All alcoholic drinks were in short supply throughout the war and a manufacturer had a ready market for as much as he could produce, albeit at a controlled price.

When the war ended, Starkey, Knight and Ford decided that their future lay in brewing beer rather than cider making. They sold Quantock Vale to Taunton Cider and Mr. Rowley persuaded Starkey's to use the same formula for their continued association with Taunton as had been successful in the case of the Oakhill Brewery. Starkey's were paid for Quantock Vale in Taunton paper, or equity shares, and, like Oakhill Brewery, were given the right to appoint a director to the Taunton Cider Board. Quantock Vale's master cider maker, Archie Baird, moved to Norton Fitzwarren and its own cider factory was shut. The success of these sole supply agreements between Taunton Cider and brewers with tied houses was to lead in the following years to the company's dramatic growth, when it entered successively into similar agreements with other national brewers and changed its marketing tactics in the 1960s and 1970s, as we will see shortly. The immediate effect was that, when, after 1945, the army camps (or some of them) closed and the conscript soldiers (or most of them) went home, Taunton Cider with its guaranteed outlets through tied houses survived with its business intact, unlike the unfortunate Messrs Pallett and Moore in 1919.

Langdons on the other hand emerged from the war with no transport business, egg-packing restricted by wartime controls, and a thriving trade in rabbits, which had grown by 1945 to as many as 10,000 a week. The rook market was less exciting, with only 200 birds a week going to London; perhaps rook pie was not as popular as had been hoped. In 1948 one London wholesaler was reported to be holding 30,000 rooks in cold storage, and there were no government-funded 'intervention' schemes to finance overproduction and pay for storage so far as rooks were concerned. There were plenty of other scandals to do with stockpiling of food, and many fortunes easily made before the practice was brought under some kind of control. Membership of the European Community in general and our participation in its Common Agricultural Policy in particular remain helpful reminders lest we forget what happens when politicians and bureaucrats try to manage demand and supply of commodity goods and services.

As we saw, Taunton Cider was incorporated as a limited company in 1921. Having been a sole trader for 40 years, in April, 1948 Mrs. Langdon incorporated her business as B.A. Langdon & Sons Ltd. She became Chairman and Managing Director, with sons Bill and Philip as directors, along with Arthur Bristow. The nationalisation of road haulage under the style of British Road Services made it difficult to re-enter the third party transport business immediately. However, if ever an industry was not cut out for the bureaucracy, overmanning, customer neglect, union control and indecision which is difficult to avoid in any publicly-owned activity, it was road haulage. Either the whole national economy would be stifled while the experiment continued or efficient private operators would have to be allowed to re-enter the business. In the event, for a long time there was a bit of both.

Eight

WHY LANGDONS WENT OUT OF RABBITS
AND BACK INTO HAULAGE

The early days in the late 1940s of the nationalisation of road transport were not seen as an intolerable burden and affront for the myriad owners of small businesses who found themselves with new titles, cash from the compensation in their pockets, comfortable salaries, and none of the hassle which comes with having to provide an efficient service for the great British public. The luxury of working fixed hours, arriving home in time for tea, mowing the lawn regularly over the weekend, even a mention in the Birthday Honours, was a novelty few of them had previously enjoyed and it is not surprising that some were quick to assume the mantle of the bureaucrat. We must also remember that many people really believed that firms which were nationalised and guided by politicians would provide the public with a better service than that which came from those actuated by the profit motive, or greed. There were many, even a majority for a while, who hoped that employees of the state would see themselves as privileged to help the public, rather than, as they soon appeared to be, monopolists whose leaders were mainly concerned about the preservation of jobs and the size of pay packets.

It was not long before producers and manufacturers needing to move goods economically and efficiently found that the service provided by the nationalised monolith was what its employees chose to deliver rather than what its customers thought they were paying for. Other than where the haulage of livestock was concerned—even Mr. Attlee dared not confront the farming lobby—all carriage of goods for hire was regulated by licence in a way designed to protect the state monopoly.

A 'C' licence, which allowed the carriage of your own goods, was not too difficult to obtain, but as it prevented any back-loading for third parties, it meant that operating costs were unnecessarily high because of so much 'running light'. A 'B' licence allowed transport of goods for hire within stated limitations, either as to distance or as to the type of goods which might be carried. No licence, not even a 'B' with restrictions, was easy to obtain, and it was not much help to be limited by law to carrying timber, for example, if all the return traffic was in foodstuffs. The 'A' licence, covering long distance haulage for third parties, was jealously guarded by the nationalised body which traded under the misleading title of British Road Services, and, even after the monopoly ended, in effect an 'A' licence could only be acquired through transfer with a vehicle, rather like the position with fishing quotas and trawlers today. It was a system designed to protect those with vested interests and make life difficult for interlopers who might challenge them, regardless of the fact that in the end all these distortions and additional costs have to be paid for by someone.

As British Road Services matured, road services to British industry became increasingly inefficient. Obviously the industry operated under a closed shop, so that any driver or manager wanting to innovate or work in the interest of customers quickly found himself stepping out of line and in hot water. Latterly the managers' problems were compounded by their having to spend many of their office hours filling in forms to oppose the increasing attacks on their monopoly, leaving even less time in which to try to run a business: and that on top of the usual form-filling and returns without which any government activity ceases to have any meaning.

By 1949, Langdons, along with every other manufacturer or producer in the land, but especially those trading in perishable goods, found it impossible to operate efficiently through relying on the nationalised carrier. That year it obtained a 'C' licence for a single lorry and bought a Seddon which was based in Wiveliscombe. The following year a second lorry was bought and based in Taunton. With the monopoly in road transport still fiercely defended by the political and industrial wings of the Labour Party, by many inside the industry whose sinecures were on the line, and by those in Whitehall whose livelihood depended on things staying as they were, there was no possibility of Langdons, or anyone else, re-entering the business of long-distance common carriers without political change.

The egg, rabbit and poultry side of the business was going well. Bill Langdon brought the chicken farm at The Larches back into production as soon as feedstuffs became available. In 1948, with the closure of the Taunton premises, all the poultry business was concentrated in Wiveliscombe and hand-plucking of birds gave way to mechanisation, allowing output to be increased from 200 a day to as many as 1,700. The leased egg-packing building was retained in Taunton until 1952 when the firm decided to replace it with a new freehold factory, which opened in February 1953. And then there were the rabbits.

We noted how Mrs. Langdon had cornered the local wild rabbit market by financing the trappers in their war against the farmers. As demand grew, so the area in which Langdons' rabbits were caught widened, and by 1955 the firm was employing eight trappers full-time in addition to the casuals, and sending to market 12,000 rabbits a week. There was no reason why the trade should not have gone on growing. Rabbit stew is toothsome and, having long been a staple diet in the countryside, the taste had been acquired by townsmen also. If you took a country stroll in the late evening, the pastures would be alive with grey bodies and white tails grazing merrily, watching the scenery or playing tag. It was not uncommon to be able count fifty or more animals in a single field. The damage they did to crops was calculated at over £50,000,000 a year in the money of those days, and that was almost certainly a wild underestimate.

Rabbits breed: they breed like ... well, it's hard to think of a suitable simile. The main flush of kittens is between January and June, but some does, or was it the bucks, didn't know the rules and kept producing all year round. A doe would have between four and eight kittens at a time, and average ten litters a year. No wonder the countryside was overrun with them, and the farmers detested them.

Brazilian rabbits had suffered from a viral disease called myxomatosis since 1898. Although victims in the wild survived, the same strain was fatal in a domestic rabbit. France, whence the rabbit had been introduced into England in the first place, suffered as great agricultural losses from the pest as its neighbour across the Channel. To combat the plague, in 1952 the French authorities introduced myxomatosis, with rapid and satisfactory results, except, of course, for the rabbit community. Nobody has admitted doing such a dastardly act as deliberately to introduce the virus into England, but in 1953 it made its appearance in the south east, and animals with gross swellings of their heads and genital parts were found sitting, dazed and dying, in the hedgerows and by the roadside. Two years later, the virus reached the west country and the rabbit population virtually disappeared. On top of that, people didn't fancy eating rabbit any more, despite official assurances that the disease affected only rabbits and hares. Perhaps they trusted authority less in those early days of the Welfare State, and were more

inclined not to take at face value official pronouncements on the possibility of transmission of a disease from an animal to a human through eating meat. It may even be
true: perhaps it is safe to eat a diseased rabbit. At all events, by 1955, the rabbit-meat
trade was dead and the Langdons had to think of something else to do if the Chiefs
were not to outnumber the Indians.

The 1950 and 1951 General Elections wiped out the large Labour majority from
1945, but failed to give either party a mandate, either to continue the faltering or failed
socialist experiment in nationalisation, or to return to a free-market system. In October
1954 the Conservative government tried to modify some of the abuses, inefficiency and
overmanning inherent in the Dock Labour Scheme and were confronted with a national
strike which damaged the economy and led to food shortages. From 26 March 1955 the
country went without its national newspapers for four weeks as the electricians under the
later discredited Communist Frank Foulkes joined with the engineering unions to shut
down the printing presses in Fleet Street. In May the railwaymen went out on strike, to
be followed soon after by the dockworkers (again). It was a mark of the general disillusion
with Labour and the unions that for some weeks the BBC toyed with objective reporting
on industrial issues, despite its own vested interest in state control.

In the midst of this chaos, Sir Anthony Eden called a general election on 27 May
1955 resulting in the return of a government with a mandate to dismantle a noble social
experiment or return some sanity to industrial life, depending on the point from which
you were looking. One of the first things it did was to allow competition in the road
transport industry by authorising the transfer of 'A' licences.

As soon as the monopoly in road haulage ended Mrs. Langdon, with her sons Bill
and Philip, enlisted the help of an experienced haulier called Sidney Pulsford who, after
his business had been nationalised, found himself unsuited to a bureaucratic existence.
The Pulsfords had been common carriers based in Langley Marsh, a village lying to the
north of Wiveliscombe, since the 18th century, moving into mechanical haulage as the
horse gave way to the lorry. By 1939 Pulsfords were a sizeable firm, with some 30
lorries carrying cattle to market and returning with animal feedstuffs. It seems odd that
Pulsfords were nationalised at all, unless Sidney decided to take the money or believed
in a socialist Utopia. At that time I was working with Gerald Harvey, who ran a similar
business from Sleaford in Lincolnshire. Mr. Harvey had no worries about being taken
over by the state and Harveys was said to have become the largest privately-owned
haulier in the country at the time.

With Mr. Pulsford's help, in 1956 Langdons established a haulage company which
was called Tone Vale Transport Ltd, based in Wiveliscombe, re-entering the business
from which they had been forced out when the war broke out in 1939—hauling
feedstuffs west from Avonmouth and carrying produce to London. Sidney Pulsford was
to stay with the firm for some years, even after losing his sight, and another former BRS
manager, Ken Thorne, was recruited to manage it.

Tone Vale Transport started with two lorries. Within two years the fleet had grown
to 17 and the firm was offering daily delivery from Cornwall to London, although why
the process took 17 hours is not something which can easily be explained. By today's
standards, the operation remained primitive. The vehicles, even when carrying perishable goods, were not temperature-controlled. The loads were carried on flat-beds, with
all the delay and labour involved in sheeting with a tarpaulin and with roping. In those
days before synthetic fibres were common, if it rained, the rope shrunk and, unless

The best of the Langdons' Fleet in 1956.

eased, might damage the load. The fork-lift truck and the pallet had appeared on the transport scene, but were not yet in common use, and drivers had to be fit and brawny enough to load and unload the vehicles, hand-balling as it is called.

In 1956 Bessie Langdon finally handed over the running of the businesses and set off to see her daughter Betty and her three grandchildren in New Zealand. She died of measles in March 1957 at the age of 76, leaving the business to her sons, Bill and Philip.

Tone Vale Transport was one leg of the Langdons' transport operation. To reveal the other we have to retrace our steps to before 1939 when a driver called Tom Hewett was driving for the Taunton family firm of Bowermans. That firm, like Pulsford's Haulage Limited, was nationalised after the war, the affable Douglas Bowerman becoming the manager of British Road Services in Taunton and a most unlikely civil servant. When Tom was demobilised in 1946, he was taken on again by Bowermans, and soon found himself working for British Road Services, with Douglas Bowerman as his ultimate boss. And so he continued until 1956, when the state's monopoly was relaxed by the Eden government. Faced with more efficient competition and a declining business, British Road Services decided to close its Taunton depot and concentrate in Bridgwater. Tom lived in Norton Fitzwarren, the other side of town, and did not want to move or travel so far. He, therefore, with Douglas Bowerman's help and encouragement, approached Arthur Forsey, a trader and haulier in Weston-super-Mare, suggesting that he might open a depot for Mr. Forsey's firm in Taunton.

Mr. Forsey had owned a tallow factory in Ricketts Lane, Weston-super-Mare, the raw materials for which were picked up from slaughterhouses around the county. From those contacts, he had also built up a useful business in meat haulage and having a depot in Taunton under someone as reliable and conscientious as Tom Hewett appealed to him. Tom arranged for Forsey's to buy two lorries with 'A' licences from British Road Services, and set up business, first in a yard with two nissen huts on a caravan site in Norton Fitzwarren and, after a few months, at the former tram depot in Taunton. (I told you we would meet it again.) For some time Tom both drove a lorry and managed the branch. He had one other driver at the start whose name will be memorable to fans of the television series *Minder*, a Londoner who proved adept at obtaining work in boxed meat from Smithfield market to provide return loads in place of the carcasses which were being brought up from the west country. Another driver to join the firm in its early days was Derek Champion, who is still with Langdons to this day.

Before long Tom and Arthur Daley (yes, it was his name) needed a third lorry and driver, in addition to which they were passing work to the operation in Weston-super-Mare. A contact in Taunton Market with Jack Biddlecombe of the fledgling Nether Stowey Meat Supply Company (from which a substantial business was to develop in time) led to the capture of regular daily loads to Smithfield market. Tom also won the business of hauling New Zealand lamb from Avonmouth docks, with an occasional cargo of butter thrown in. Before long he was spending much of his time as a salesman and administrator in addition to driving, and was operating for Mr. Forsey out of Taunton a fleet of five vehicles in the meat trade, although none of them was refrigerated.

At this juncture, with the business outgrowing its resources in the tram depot, first Mr. Forsey and then his son, John, urged Tom Hewett to relocate his activity in Weston-super-Mare. In effect Tom was the business and he was as reluctant to move for them as he had been for his friend Douglas Bowerman. As Tom wouldn't budge, the Forseys agreed to help him go into business on his own account. On 23 August 1960 he wrote to Mr. Forsey agreeing to buy three lorries, together with their 'A' licences, 'totalling a tonnage of 10 tons 14 cwt 3 qrs' for the current market value which was also to include the depot lease, a fuel pump, a tyre pump and office equipment and 'a new set of tyres for VYB 159'. Forsey replied two days later to the effect that 'to the best of our knowledge and belief, the weight of the three Special "A" licences total 10 ton 7 cwt 28 lbs': but what were seven hundredweight and two quarters between friends? The deal was duly consummated, but without the Forseys being aware that Tom was about to be financed by Langdons, who would in effect gain control of its operations, with Tom as a director and manager. On 26 September 1960, Taunton Meat Haulage Ltd was incorporated, the initial papers showing that Tom and the company secretary of Tone Vale Transport Ltd had a share each. The eventual directors were Tom Hewett, Sidney Pulsford and Philip Langdon but the majority shareholder was not Tom Hewett.

Now the Langdon body had two legs, Tone Vale Transport Ltd hauling ambient loads based in Wiveliscombe with Kenneth Thorne, running it mainly under Bill Langdon's direction, and Taunton Meat Haulage Limited with Tom as manager but Philip Langdon effectively in control. Bill was an engineer, more interested in the mechanical side of the business, always ready to turn out if there was a breakdown. Philip was a keen businessman, with an awareness of Tom's ability to deliver results in a difficult trade. Although there was a certain amount of sub-contracting from Taunton to Wiveliscombe, it would be some time before the two transport companies under the same ownership were amalgamated as Langdons.

Nine

How Langdons Survived Fire and Strikes, Bill Langdon Died and Philip Sold the Business

Bessie Langdon was an exceptional person. She proved herself an astute businesswoman who succeeded in what was then very much a man's world, and brought up a family as well. She could be strict, and nobody was allowed to utter any oath in her presence. She was wise enough while she remained fit in body and mind to hand over her business to two capable, if different, brothers who were to remain partners until death parted them. The third member of the triumvirate was Sidney Pulsford, whom we met briefly a few pages back.

Bill Langdon, the once farmer, short-term emigrant to Canada and always engineer, was liked and respected by all the people who worked for and with him. His younger brother, Philip, was a keen businessman and took the harder decisions over discipline, upon which Bill would usually plead that the culprit should be given another chance. You have to be fairly rugged to work in the transport and distribution business, whether as a driver, as a warehouseman or as a manager, and Bill may well have needed his more pragmatic younger brother beside him if the business were to prosper. Bill, it would appear, disliked confrontation whereas Philip was not someone to be pushed around, and especially by any trade-union official.

In retrospect it seems odd that the Langdon brothers kept the two businesses, Taunton Meat Haulage and Tone Vale Transport, apart under different managers, Ken Thorne and Tom Hewett, even to the extent of running separate repair garages, a division which was perpetuated by Philip after Bill's death. There was not in those days the sharp divide between temperature-controlled and ambient haulage which has since developed. Promoting a single brand and sharing resources, especially tractors, repair facilities and traffic control, would have seemed a logical development. On the other hand, the two brothers were different in temperament, and they may have decided it would be better for each to run his own show.

Before making any adverse criticism, we should not forget that the 1960s and 1970s were difficult days for employers and employees alike. Powerful trade union leaders like Hugh (Lord) Scanlon, Frank Cousins, and Jack Jones in effect guided their executives and their conferences, which decided policy and attracted as delegates the more extreme members. The unions and their officials enjoyed immunity from damages for breaches of contract even when a strike was used as a political weapon, involved secondary picketing or was called without notice in defiance of agreement. Any unionist who failed to obey instructions to strike faced the loss of his card, and so of his livelihood. A closed shop obliged all employees to belong to the union, and denied them a job if they didn't. It is not surprising that some union leaders repeatedly led their troops into battle in what sometimes appeared to outsiders as much a political war as an industrial one. Even those with no political ambitions were unwilling or unable to control the 'unofficial' activities of the likes of Derek Robinson ('Red Robbo'), Jack Dash and many other like-minded, intransigent or undisciplined local officials. Unhappily there was only one George Woodcock. When on television I, as a token employer, had to debate with him, as General Secretary of the TUC, I found it impossible to disagree with him. It can't have made for riveting viewing.

In the face of a government which was sympathetic or in thrall to the unions, some employers kept their heads down and concentrated on running their concerns with as little disruption as possible. Others allowed themselves to be pushed into confrontation, and those were the ones whose businesses suffered more and whose employees often lost their jobs. It was a climate in which the coward survived—but at such a cost. What, I wonder, would Mr. Dash make of his London Docklands today? We will shortly see what effect this climate of industrial ill-temper had on Taunton Meat Haulage.

The Langdon brothers carried on the chicken and egg business for a few years after their mother's death, although, as in the brewing industry, the emergence of large-scale producers with national distribution made life difficult for the family firms. It was almost inevitable that, in 1955, the Wiveliscombe brewer, Arnold and Hancock, should be taken over, as it was by Ushers of Trowbridge. We shall be looking more closely at the effect of these brewery mergers in the context of Taunton Cider. They were only justified in financial terms if local production ceased and brewing was concentrated centrally: the attraction for the predator was access to the tied houses of the victim, not his production facilities nor the brand of beer he sold. Like so many others up and down the country, the Wiveliscombe brewery was closed, following what was considered a decent interval of three years after the takeover, along with its cider-making facilities. Some of the brewery staff were transferred to the other Arnold and Hancock brewery in Taunton, but that too was also shut down before very long.

The rest found themselves out of work.

In 1960, the Langdon brothers bought the extensive buildings and grounds which Arnold and Hancock had occupied in Wiveliscombe. This purchase enabled them to relocate their chicken processing business in the former brewery, to provide in the former cider factory a warehouse for a storage business which they called the West Somerset Warehousing Company, and to move the repair workshops for Tone Vale Transport out of Church Street on to the same site. Before long, they were employing more than 200 people in chicken processing alone, managed by Bill's son, Peter Langdon, who had been born on New Year's Day, 1936. The threat to employment in the small town seemed to have receded. It was, however, proving increasingly difficult to make money in poultry and in 1962 they sold the operation, with the buildings it occupied, to the Ross Group, one of whose first actions was to dismiss Peter and install their own manager. The Langdon brothers also sold the farm at The Larches and the egg-packing business in Taunton and this is the last sighting we will have of Langdons as egg and poultry producers. After the disposal to Ross, the brothers kept a large part of the brewery's land and buildings, including the warehouse in the former cider house.

West Somerset Warehousing Company prospered in its new premises, developing a substantial business in storing cardboard cartons for the Tiverton firm of John Heathcoat and aerosols for a leading manufacturer in Wellington. It also transported eggs in the old Langdon tradition, and, of all things, basic slag. To stay with it for a moment, we can note that all went well for some years until 15 September 1969, when the old cider house, and its contents, were destroyed in an inferno made more dramatic by aerosol cans exploding like the sound of gunfire. The firemen from Dulverton, Wellington and Taunton joined their Wiveliscombe brethren to watch a conflagration which none of them could put out, and the entire property was gutted. Not surprisingly, Heathcoat's and Aerosols Ltd were unhappy about the loss of their inventory and, when West

Somerset Warehousing relocated on the site of the old SRD in Norton Fitzwarren, those two customers took their business elsewhere.

A small town like Wiveliscombe is always at risk if it depends on one or two large employers. Neither Ross's, nor their successors, were able to make profits in the chicken-processing business, which was closed altogether in 1973. The blow was especially hard on the townsfolk because the venerable weaving firm, owned by the Wellington Quaker Fox family (whom we last met as bankers), also closed its Wiveliscombe factory that year, leaving another 200 people without work. Closures like this send shock-waves through a community. Among those who lost their businesses in the aftermath of the two sets of redundancy was Bill's son, Peter, who had established a grocery business in the town. He at least was able to go back to driving a Heavy Goods Vehicle.

I don't plan to confuse you, or myself, with an analysis of all the companies the Langdons owned and who became director when of which. Until 1981 when the Langdon transport and storage businesses (or most of them) came together on the site of an old sugar warehouse at Walford Cross, four miles out of Taunton on the way to Bridgwater, there were in effect always two Langdons' camps, the Taunton Meat Haulage men and the Wiveliscombe crowd. Even today, some eccentricity in a Langdons' employee may be explained by a knowing wink and a reminder that the person concerned hailed from Wiveliscombe.

The two halves of the transport business stayed with their respective markets, one having refrigerated vehicles and the other flatbeds for the carriage of goods at ambient temperatures, although sometimes the Tone Vale trucks would attach an insulated box on the flatbed to help out Taunton Meat Haulage. Some of the goods carried by Tone Vale Transport, like cheese or butter, would today need temperature-controlled vehicles, but in those days the public had a stronger resistance to food impurity than it does today, despite the efforts of the Food Hygiene and Public Health officials to monitor and regulate everything.

The daily service which Tone Vale Transport operated from Cornwall to London carried eggs and other foodstuffs, with return loads mainly of agricultural feedstuffs and, latterly, artificial fertilisers. Later Tone Vale established a close connection with the Watchet-based Wansborough Paper Company, involving storage as well as carriage. The icing was taken off that cake, however, when the paper company bought its own transport business, Griggs, and later on the storage was lost to a competitor when the Langdons' warehouse supervisor, operating in a remote shed in the old SRD at Norton Fitzwarren, decided that his tea breaks and those of his staff should not be interrupted by telephone calls from Watchet and left the phone off the hook. By the time his manager knew about it, the work had gone elsewhere, as did the supervisor and his staff soon afterwards.

Taunton Meat Haulage under Tom Hewett soon outgrew its premises in the old tram depot and in 1965 the firm was relocated a couple of miles out of town down the A38 on the edge of the village of Bathpool in what is now a wholesale tyre depot. An adjacent garage which sold Regent petrol was owned by a small national chain operating under the name Blue Star or Super Star. The Langdon brothers bought this business too and would have acquired the Mercedes agency for the district had they been able to agree terms of the stocking of demonstrator cars and the level of spares. I had a week or two previously agreed to buy the property for someone else for, if memory serves me right, the sum of £17,500 and this was the first time I came across what was later called gazumping.

The most important slice of business Tom Hewett won for Taunton Meat Haulage was the work of the substantial Willand abattoir, Lloyd Maunder, hauling several loads of meat every day to London. Well, not every day, because of the strikes: but everyone became used to the occasional 'day of action', in fact a day of inaction, during which the majority of workers took an unwanted day off without pay. Across the town at the engineering company, Avimo Ltd, the management persuaded those who wanted to work on the day of the strike to stay away, and in return the whole labour force would come in on normal rates the following Sunday, to make up lost production. The BBC would duly announce to the world how solid the engineers' strike had been in Taunton, and so everyone got what they wanted.

Despite the 'English disease' of constant strikes, the Langdon businesses were making solid progress when Bill Langdon suddenly died on 5 April 1967. The brothers had agreed that the survivor should take over the entire company in the event of the death of either, and Philip duly paid his sister-in-law the sum of £15,000 to become the sole owner of Langdons. Bill's son, Peter (the former grocer), was voted off the Boards of the various Langdon companies and Sidney Pulsford also left. Philip was now in sole charge, with Tom Hewett continuing to manage the Taunton operation on a day-to-day basis, and Ken Thorne the Wiveliscombe end.

Despite Bill's death, the transport businesses continued to expand. Philip bought a number of 'A' licences from the Wellington hauliers, Kerslakes, and then the company G. Champion Limited in Barnstaple, with its yard and seven vehicles which carried mainly coal, scrap metal and sheepskins. A few months later he closed the operation in Barnstaple, selling the yard and transferring the fleet to Wiveliscombe.

At Taunton Meat Haulage in Bathpool relations with the drivers, their union and a local union official were not at all happy. The position was exacerbated by what seems to have been an ill-advised attempt by the management to cut the drivers' meal allowance by two shillings a day. That was worth much more than its present equivalent, 10p, but hardly, it might seem in retrospect, a *casus belli*. But who are we to judge, with the Thatcher reforms behind us? The union threatened a strike if the cut was made and Philip Langdon told the drivers that, if they went on strike, they would be sacked. They did and they were. The biggest customer, Lloyd Maunder, decided, as Bessie Langdon had in 1926, that strikes in the carrier on whom their business depended were bad news and it had better make other arrangements for its transport. Taunton Meat Haulage lost the lion's share of their business, the striking drivers lost their jobs, and everyone became worse off as a result.

From then on, relations between management and drivers in Taunton Meat Haulage remained unsettled. There was still work at Avonmouth, carrying New Zealand lamb and butter away from the docks. The butter went on unrefrigerated lorries, and nobody seems to have complained. The frozen lamb would sometimes be off-loaded by the stevedores on to the quay, where it would be left in the heat or sun for several hours while they waited around until they could start working on overtime rates. All a driver could do was watch helplessly while his load became more and more soggy and a candidate for rejection at its final destination. As for the port management: well, there wasn't much, and what there was was ineffective. This was the world of the closed shop and the Dock Labour Scheme. If you wanted to find management in a

A Taunton Meat Haulage refrigerated rig in 1970. Trevor Horton recalls painting the livery by hand in the workshop.

port, you had to go to Felixstowe, or Exmouth, or any place where the Scheme was not operative.

(Prior to the 1979 election, which Mrs. (Baroness) Thatcher won, I was asked to appear in a televised discussion with a representative from the Bristol dockers about industrial relations in general and the Dock Labour Scheme in particular. They made my point for me by sending six shop stewards to the studio for the transmission.)

In 1974 the economy was in a bad state, taxes were high, the unions were intransigent and above the law, trade was poor, and Langdons were not making much money. Running a privately-owned business without a partner to share the burden is difficult when things are going well, and debilitating when they are not. Philip Langdon decided that it was time to sell and, after abortive talks with a firm in Southampton, agreed terms in April 1974 with a conglomerate called Price and Pierce. As the new owner left him in charge virtually as before, and changed nothing in the running of the firm, we can defer taking a closer look at who they were and what they did with their new purchase until they themselves passed into the hands of another owner, who was prepared to take an active interest in Langdons. In the meanwhile, for all those who worked in the Langdon companies, Philip Langdon remained in charge.

In addition to work from Avonmouth Docks and for local abattoirs, Tom Hewett built up a substantial trade carrying meat into Europe, with horses from Ireland being a particular stand-by for the French and Belgian *chevaline* market, to support which an office had been established in Dublin. Another regular item of outward traffic was frozen eggs, with Italian fruit, Belgian paté, Dutch yoghurt and French butter for Sainsburys making up the usual return loads. However, the fraught atmosphere between the company and the continental drivers did not make for an efficient operation. The company considered the drivers were fiddling their expenses, which was why the operation was not making any money. The drivers, whose attitude to expenses and time-sheets may well have been somewhat cavalier, were equally unhappy with the management. In the spring of 1975, the union was again threatening a strike at Langdons (apart from the national stoppages) and Philip Langdon, with the backing of his new owners, decided he had had enough. Acting with great care to ensure that none of the vehicles remained out of the country when he announced his decision, all the drivers in Taunton Meat Haulage were dismissed, to be replaced by owner-drivers. The meat traffic from Ireland was abandoned, the Dublin office

A Tone Vale Transport flat-bed in the 1970s, showing lots of roping and a rather tatty tarpaulin.

was closed and the company Langdons had registered in Ireland, Eurofrigo Ltd, was itself put into cold storage.

The owner-driver concept had been developed by a company operating ready-mix concrete lorries, and is said to have originated in Australia, which, in those dark days, shared with the Mother Country a reputation for powerful and difficult transport unions. Roy Hutchings, who was then the Finance Director of Taunton Meat Haulage, had worked in the ready-mixed concrete business and suggested that Philip Langdon should adopt the same scheme. What happens is that the driver buys his tractor, often with financial assistance or backing from the haulier. The haulier keeps the driver's accounts and finds loads for him in the haulier's trailers. The driver normally receives the price which the customer is charged for the haulage, but pays a commission to the haulier for the services which he provides, including the use of the trailers. The advantage for the driver is that he can build up an equity in his vehicle and eventually genuinely go into business on his own, as several Langdons' drivers have done with considerable success. The advantage for the haulier is that the driver works harder on his own account than as an employee, takes more care of his own vehicle, has to find the money to buy the vehicle and doesn't go on strike. The disadvantage for the driver is that initially he has to incur debt and that he has little security of employment, because he is given virtually no time in which to work for a third party. The disadvantage for the haulier is that owner-drivers like to cherry-pick, leaving the less profitable jobs with empty running to the company drivers. The disadvantage for the state is that the employer does not have to pay the tax on employment called National Insurance because the driver is self-employed.

When Taunton Meat Haulage sacked its 15 or 16 drivers in 1975, Philip Langdon had laid his plans well. An army sergeant instructor called Ron Blake had been moonlighting as a driver for the company while stationed at Norton Fitzwarren. He retired from the army and became one of the first owner-drivers. Peter Langdon had been one of the original drivers in 1966 to undertake its continental traffic, before managing the chicken processing plant and the grocery venture. He too became an owner-driver. Others, famous names in Langdons' lore, followed suit, especially Derek Champion (whom we last met in the tram terminus), Maxie Mehrlich and Gordon Ardren, who retired as an owner-driver in the summer of 1999 and immediately returned to work as a company driver. All five are still closely associated with Langdons and are part of its history.

With plenty of cheap accommodation to rent in the old SRD at Norton Fitzwarren, Price and Pierce decided in 1975 to sell the garage in Bathpool and to relocate Taunton Meat Haulage in the SRD. The building which they rented for the workshops was fairly unprepossessing and the office was in a Portacabin; but there was lots of room for parking, and no investment in real estate. Following its fire in the old cider house, West Somerset Warehousing joined them at Norton, with one of its sheds there dedicated to the storage of fertilisers for ICI. In 1964 Tone Vale Transport had also moved out of the brewery, although it stayed in Wiveliscombe, with a garage in new premises in Ford Road. There it maintained its own lorries as well doing work for some of those belonging to two other companies, Solent Shipping and Transport, and Trevone Properties, one of which shared Ken Thorne as a director and the other being connected with the Langdon family, but outside the sale to Price and Pierce.

Talking to the many Langdons' employees still with the company who worked for the firm during those years, you get the impression that they were justifiably apprehensive about the future. Difficulties with Solent Shipping and Transport following the death of its manager Jack Fassett may well have been a contributory cause in the deterioration of Ken Thorne's health. Philip Langdon himself, doing a lonely job, was not universally popular with the staff. These were frustrating days for any manager. The Labour government seemed bent on making life difficult for them and had once again become convinced that a panacea for its woes lay in more nationalisation. In 1977, despite the parlous state of the economy, parliament, with no doubt the noblest intentions, voted to nationalise the aircraft and shipbuilding industries: aircraft was to survive the experiment but shipbuilding did not. It is difficult to recall two decades later precisely how often the steel industry passed into and out of public ownership at that time, but the game of ping-pong played with it by the politicians was disastrous for the industry and for those who worked in it.

In March 1977, 40,000 workers at British Leyland were laid off because of a strike by toolmakers. In July, an attempted bribe, sop or reward from the political to the industrial wing of the Labour party under the name 'The Social Contract' proved as ineffective as all other pleas for restraint in wage demands had done. In July also the railwaymen showed their contempt for their government and society by lodging a 63 per cent wage claim, threatening to strike if it was not met. In November a strike blacked out the opening of parliament. And so it went.

It was not surprising that anyone trying to manage a business in those troubled days should have been frustrated. Personal tax was levied at 83 per cent, with an additional 15 per cent on investment income, and, one year, a further retrospective surcharge took the total over 100 per cent. The union leaders, with a few courageous exceptions, used their power with little apparent thought for the national good, or indeed the long-term interest of their members, who were seldom consulted about strikes anyway. It was enough to induce any proprietor of a private business in the mid-1970s to sell up and take life more easily. As we see, Philip Langdon had sold, but he had to stay with the business. If there is one thing harder than becoming an effective non-executive Chairman of a business of which you have been Chief Executive, it is continuing to run for another a business which you previously owned. Unfortunately a buyer may not allow a vendor just to walk away. In a sense, Philip Langdon was trapped.

Ten

How Taunton Cider Became Big Business

Our last look at Taunton Cider was in the period just after the Second World War when the horizons for what had hitherto been a small, mainly local, business had been widened first by the supply agreements with Oakhill Brewery and then with Starkey, Knight and Ford. The attempt to penetrate the market in the south east had not been successful, you will recall, with the closure of the bottling plant under the arches in Harrow. What a modern Public Health Inspector may have thought of that location is not for us to speculate.

Serious practical difficulties faced any small cider maker wanting to expand. As we noted earlier, there is the question of taste: cider drinkers become used to what is available locally, from the apple trees in the neighbourhood. Perfectly good cider made from a different variety of trees may be deemed unpalatable. To overcome this prejudice, customers have to be educated into recognising a special flavour in the branded drink, which must then be the same in every outlet and from month to month. The taste also has to be different from what can be made locally, because distribution and marketing will cost more than the local product, and the price therefore has to be higher. H.P.Bulmer of Hereford was the first company to recognise and develop this market, and by 1970 it had gained 65 per cent of the cider trade nationally.

Taunton Cider knew that, if it were to grow, it had to come up with something different from its standard draught product, and in 1955 it produced a dry bottled cider for which it chose the brand name *Natch*. It was not until 1964 that a deal was struck, which we will mention in due time, leading to the acquisition of another blend of cider with the more charismatic name of *Autumn Gold*.

Another difficulty to be overcome in gaining wider market acceptance was the price the customer had to pay. As Mrs. Beeton showed us, and every countryman knew anyway, anyone can make cider. For them, the raw materials cost little or nothing. All they need is access to a cider press or, failing that, a strong plastic bag with holes in it or a sack, in which to squeeze the fruit and collect the juice; and then, patience while the natural chemicals in the skin of the fruit accomplish the process of fermentation. In the west country especially, every farm had its vast barrels of local cider in the cellar or an outhouse and, even if the farmer didn't make it himself, it was very cheap to buy in bulk, being free of excise duty.

A third marketing problem was social acceptability. Despite the eminence of many of the Victorian customers of Heathfield Rectory, cider remained a labourer's tipple and a Cider House, like Taunton's last surviving example in Upper High Street, was a rough-and-tumble, down-at-heel, spit-and-sawdust sort of place. Men with cash in their pocket and a thirst preferred beer; respectable women, however rich or thirsty, were not much seen in public houses. The wider market for any branded cider sold over the bar would not develop until a more affluent pub-going drinker could be induced to order it on a regular basis. That meant persuading women, especially teenagers, to drink it, and suggesting that, despite its alcoholic content, it was also a healthy drink for children. It was not for nothing that the marketing men chose to describe *Autumn Gold* as a 'family cider'.

Fortunately, the 'social acceptability' barrier was broken down by the enterprise of two other small firms, who between them persuaded women that they could go into a pub without demeaning themselves or falling prey to the lascivious lusts of men by drinking beer, wine or spirits; and then that there was a ladylike alcoholic drink which they could sip without risking eternal damnation. The first innovator started operating just after the war from a former egg packing station, known locally as the Egg Factory, on a footpath between Victoria Road and Arbour Lane in the parish of Springfield on the outskirts of Chelmsford in Essex. The footpath was known as the 'Bunny Walk', from the profusion of rabbits to be seen in the water meadows beside the River Can, their life undisturbed by the distant Mrs. Langdon and her trappers. Inside the Egg Factory, a female staff pierced seven-pound tins of imported fruit juice, and poured the contents into small bottles, which the proprietor then sold to local publicans who were thus able to offer the female companions of their male customers a non-alcoholic drink. As a further touch, it was suggested that the fruit juice had been enriched with vitamins, as indeed it may have been. The company called itself British Vitamin Products, or Britvic for short, and we will meet it again when it had long outgrown the Egg Factory.

The other innovators were the Showering family in Shepton Mallet, Somerset, who owned a small cider and perry business. The perry, or fermented pear juice, was an alcoholic drink which, like Britvic, was packed in small, or 'baby', bottles to be drunk by women in pubs, and was marketed as 'Champagne Perry': not a bad name, but, like Taunton Cider's 'Natch', not that catchy either. The story goes that during a Board meeting, one of the drivers put his head round the door seeking delivery instructions for a load of the baby bottles of champagne perry, which he described as baby-chams. As the Bard said, what's in a name? In marketing, quite a lot. We will also meet Showerings again.

The biggest obstacle for any small cider seeking to break into the big time was the competition offered by Bulmers, the runaway market leader, followed by Gaymers of Attleborough in Norfolk, Whiteways of Whimple in Devon, Sheppeys also in Somerset, Showerings, Coates—there were so many of them, with their special tie-ups, brand names and adherents. In addition, the competitors had protected certain features with registered designs or patents, some of which might seem not to have been 'true and original inventions' to an outsider. An example was Coates's exclusive right to sell cider in a registered design of half-gallon pitchers with integral handles despite the fact that the Greeks were using the same pattern to contain their wine in classical times and no self-respecting Roman galleon can be excavated from its long stay on the bed of the Mediterranean Sea without disgorging its cargo of similar amphorae.

Yet Taunton Cider Ltd had one distinction: its exclusive supply agreement with two breweries and their tied houses, which, for most of its production, cut out all selling and marketing costs. Certainly the brewers bought the product at a discount of 8 per cent compared with other customers, to reflect this economy, but at least there was an assured market, without having to go head-to-head nationally with well-entrenched competitors. There was also a useful local trade, looked after by company salesmen rather than an agent after the retirement in the 1950s of the former pulse-grower and publican, Mr. Jeanes; of him it can be truly said, despite his failure with the peas, he had his finger on the pulse of the local licensed trade.

All was running smoothly in the early 1960s. Taunton Cider remained a small business, with a turnover of no more than £500,000, buying from local orchards, employing people in Norton Fitzwarren and making a modest profit for its owners. This happy state of affairs was to be changed, but not threatened, by an orgy of takeovers and amalgamations in the brewing industry, which could only be justified financially if economies of scale followed. As with Arnold and Hancock in Wiveliscombe, after an amalgamation local breweries had to be closed and real ales (which needed looking after) replaced by a bland pasteurised imitation served under gas pressure from a keg, which kept better and required no skill from the publican except to wash the pipes out once a week. Similarly it made financial sense to replace local cider production with supplies from a reliable central source, and preferably under an own-brand label to keep the clientele coming back to the tied houses. However regrettable these developments may have been for the nation's serious beer drinkers, they couldn't have suited Taunton Cider better, so long as its management stuck to its knitting and avoided direct confrontation with Bulmers.

The amalgamations affected all Taunton Cider's brewery customers, actual and prospective. I won't bore you with the details except to follow through what happened to our old friends, The Oakhill Brewery, and to Starkey, Knight and Ford, the two firms whose tied houses were already supplied from Norton Fitzwarren.

The Oakhill Brewery, at Oakhill in Somerset, had been founded in 1767, and amalgamated with Bristol United Breweries in July 1925. Brewing ceased at Oakhill on the outbreak of war in 1939. Bristol United Breweries had been founded in 1889 to take over seven smaller brewers in Bristol. In 1956, owning some 600 tied houses, it was taken over by Bristol Brewery Georges and Company Ltd, which had been founded in 1788. In turn, that company was taken over in 1961 by Courage, Barclay and Company, better known as Courages.

Starkey, Knight and Ford was first registered as a company in Bridgwater (without the Ford) in 1887. It bought Thomas Ford of Tiverton in April 1895 and was in turn swallowed up with its two breweries and 400 pubs by Whitbread in 1962.

As a result of these mergers, Courages and Whitbread started to draw their cider supplies for their vast chains of public houses nationwide from Norton Fitzwarren. The traffic was not to pass all in one direction; when Grand Metropolitan, who had an exclusive contract with Bulmers, took over Watneys in the early 1970s, Taunton Cider lost a substantial part of its business, which led later to decisions being taken which, in retrospect, may look less wise than they seemed to some at the time. We can all be wise after the event: it is a testimony to the character and sagacity of Miles Roberts, whom we meet shortly, that he was wise before and during it, recognising the prime importance of Taunton Cider's recruiting, and nourishing, and retaining its brewer-shareholders.

The Courage relationship became closer in 1963 when it bought 61,450 shares in Taunton Cider for £116,272, or £1.89 a share. Courage had its own cider business, Ashford Valley in Kent, which had been part of Ashford Breweries, which had been taken over by Style and Winch in 1912 who were taken over by Barclay Perkins in 1929 who were later taken over by Courage. Courages had agreed to sell the Ashford Valley cider business to Bulmers when it realised that Bristol Brewery Georges, which it had just acquired, had a stake in Taunton Cider and a director on the Board. The deal with Bulmer was stopped, Ashford Valley was closed, and its equipment was transferred to Norton Fitzwarren for £22,000.

In 1964 the brewers in Chard and Yeovil, Brutton, Mitchell Toms, were taken over by Charringtons. Bruttons had produced their own cider—the *Autumn Gold* we noted above—and suggested to Charringtons that they should shut down the cider factory and copy what Courages had done. As a result Charrington bought 41,300 shares in Taunton Cider for £99,120, of which £46,824 was in respect of the *Autumn Gold* assets. The price of the share was now £2.40. Because Bruttons had formerly supplied cider to Ushers of Trowbridge, Ind Coope and Whitbread, they too agreed to take their cider from Taunton.

In 1965 Miles Roberts, who had been on the Board of Taunton Cider since 1954, working on the distribution side and negotiating these national agreements, was appointed its Managing Director. He was determined to strengthen and augment the links with brewers whose tied houses and off-licence trade had proved so beneficial to the operation in Norton Fitzwarren, and to exploit the company's prime position in this market rather than try to go head-to-head with Bulmers with branded products. After the Ashford Valley equipment was installed, along with other improvements, the bottling capacity in Norton Fitzwarren had been trebled to 400 half-pints an hour. In 1965 a further 1,000 dozen capacity was added.

It might appear that serendipity had brought Courage and Whitbread into the Taunton fold. Mr. Roberts decided to rely no longer on chance, and approached other brewers with an invitation for them to join the consortium, buying shares, appointing a director and, of course, taking their supplies of cider from Norton Fitzwarren. Watneys had bought Ushers of Trowbridge in May 1960 and agreed to join the consortium in 1966, buying 41,300 shares at £2.50 each. Hall and Woodhouse in Blandford Forum and Wadworth of Devizes then joined, bringing over 300 pubs with them. Eventually the list of participants in the consortium was also to include such celebrated names (to a connoisseur of ale) as Bass, Eldridge Pope, Greene King, Guinness, Heavitree, Palmers of Bridport, Scottish and Newcastle, Shepherd Neame, Tolly Cobbold and Youngs. By 1970 the firm was producing 4.7 million gallons of cider a year, and its annual turnover had trebled over six years to £1.5m.

Everything had grown—turnover, profit, employee numbers, everything except the availability of apples. The total English crop is about 250,000 tons, of which Norton Fitzwarren needed, at that rate of production, about 70,000 tons. The fruit-growing industries in France and Italy are better organised than they are in the United Kingdom. Prime quality apples are usually marketed through cooperatives, and lesser quality fruit, rather than being left to rot, is sold for chutney, pickle and other food applications: and, of course, for cider-making. When Norton Fitzwarren first became dependent on foreign apples for its production, the apples were generally imported through Exmouth in Devon, in an attempt to evade nosy people who wanted to know where the shipments were going: or at least, in the hope that someone might think they were going to a competitor nearer the port, like Whiteways. Later, it became more economical to import apple juice rather than apples, then concentrated apple juice, and then purified concentrated juice from which the natural fermentation agents had been removed. But we are now moving ahead rather too fast, and a long way from our starting point in Heathfield Rectory.

Another side of the business which had to grow was that concerned with distribution, which we will also come to in due time.

All seemed to be going splendidly in 1970 when Allied Breweries, in which Showerings were by now a major force, entered into talks to join the Taunton consortium. It is a common mistake in business to think that your competitor will stand idly by while you eat into his market share. While Taunton had been expanding its tied outlets, Bulmers had been promoting national brands to the extent that the 'own label' products from Norton Fitzwarren were no longer what many customers asked for at the bar. It was largely because of this development that the talks with Allied broke down. In addition, after years of spectacular growth, the Taunton share of the national market actually fell in 1971 to below 15 per cent.

The Taunton Cider Board, now enlarged, strengthened also perhaps, with its directors appointed by the associated breweries, decided that it would have to change its policy and establish its own brands, in addition to *Natch* and *Autumn Gold*. In 1971 Guinness, without any pubs of its own but with great brand awareness, bought 61,450 shares for £1 million, at an average price of £16.27. Their participation marked a turning point in the fortunes of Taunton Cider and the village of Norton Fitzwarren, and gives us an opportunity to take a break and another look at what else was going on in the district.

Eleven

HOW TAUNTON MOVED INTO THE MOTOR AGE
AND TRADERS MOVED OUT OF TOWN

TAUNTON, a municipal borough, the county town of Somerset, England, stands on the river Tone 45 mls SW. of Bristol … From the 14th century Taunton shared in the prosperity of the west of England woollen industry, and something of its wealth can be seen in the surviving portions of the churches of St Mary's and St James's. In 1522 Richard Fox, bishop of Winchester, founded a grammar school for boys.

The strategic importance of Taunton was shown in the royalist-parliamentary struggle, when the town withstood three sieges, being ably defended by Robert Blake (afterwards admiral). Taunton is also associated with the rebellion of the duke of Monmouth, who declared himself king of England in what was then the town's market-place on 23 June 1685; on Monmouth's defeat, Judge Jeffreys held trials in the great hall of Taunton castle on 18-19 September.

Taunton is an important market centre for the rich agricultural centre in which it stands. Its main industries comprise the manufacture of clothing (notably collars, neckties, shirts and gloves), silk, rayon, and leather, chart printing and general engineering. The town gives its name to a parliamentary constituency. S.J.J.

Chambers's Encyclopaedia (1973), Volume XIII, p.471

It is instructive to compare the above entry with the one a century earlier which confronted you at the start of Chapter I. We can ignore the historical bits, and the fact that during the 99 years between the two editions, Taunton seems to have moved a mile further away from Bristol. The Victorian contributor referred to and recognised the significance of the railway communication which the town enjoyed: his modern counterpart (Mr. S.J. James, M.A., Head of the Geography Department at St Andrew's, no less) preferred to draw our attention to its strategic importance militarily in the 17th century. The first entry told us that the woollen and silk factories had almost wholly departed: the later one refers to the manufacture of silk as one of the main industries, along with collars, gloves, rayon, leather, chart printing and general engineering. The eminent geographer was right about the shirts and ties, but not about much else in the industrial line.

I suppose you could say that 'chart-printing' took place, although the marine hydrographers who record the mysteries and perils of the deep at the Admiralty Hydrographic Establishment might have preferred a more fulsome description of the nature of their duties. Someone does indeed print charts once their navigational and cerebral labours are complete. For a time Taunton Meat Haulage used to deliver them to the Admiralty in London in the same containers as the carcasses of beef, hogs and mutton, until the customer realised that the occasional dark red stain on the oceans was not an indication of the Imperial Sun Never Setting but a result of bloody carelessness on the part of the carrier.

As for silk factories—yes, James Pearsall still used silk to make surgical sutures, and a small amount of rayon also. Avimo, which was by then one of the leading electro-optical design and manufacturing companies in Europe, could have felt justifiably miffed to be dismissed as 'general engineers'. As for Van Heusen's, the separate collars, which men fixed to their shirts with studs and changed daily, had passed almost entirely out of fashion in the early '70s. The Taylor's glove factory had also suffered from the fact that very few people wore gloves any longer and its premises were converted into a china emporium, originally specialising in the sale of manufacturers' seconds but soon turning into a more general and prosperous business.

Instead of carping further, let us take a look at what was changing in the town since our last glance at it just after the war.

One significant factor in the industrial development of the district was the release by the army in the late 1960s of its huge Supply Reserve Depot (SRD) in Norton Fitzwarren, which we have come across a few times already. Another was the fact that the Portman family had paid substantial death duties in the 1920s by handing its estate in and around Taunton over to the Crown. Prior to the release of the SRD, the only land allocated by the Borough Council for industrial development was either in a swamp or on the site of a former brickyard which had been subject to landfill. Neither location was suitable for the installation of modern machinery, which requires a firm bed and low humidity. As we noted, in the mid-1960s Avimo had to locate part of its production in Barnstaple while it entered into the laborious process of persuading the 'planners' (after two appeals) that it would not damage the nature of the town irreparably to build a modern plant in which local people could find productive employment in an industry paying high wages and using advanced technology. It finally succeeded in opening its new factory in Taunton in 1969 and was at last able to assemble delicate instruments in dust- and vibration-free conditions which had not been characteristic of its old factory beside the railway, the site now being used not for industrial enterprise but for housing.

Fortunately the Crown Commissioners decided in the 1970s to develop some of their Portman land for industrial purposes and, being above the law, did not have to obtain planning permission, thereby outflanking the defence in depth at which planning officers are so adept. Their first tenant was James Pearsall in a purpose-built factory and other firms soon followed on to the Priorswood estate. The County Council had some consolation for this lese-majesty when it rehoused its fire-fighting headquarters in the Portman family mansion at Hestercombe, where it remains to this day overlooking the magnificent gardens laid out by Lutyens and Jekyll.

We are more concerned here with transport and communications, and with cider, than with other industries, as perhaps we might have expected a geographer to have been. A student of those years is fortunate that, for all its other wasted efforts, the South West Economic Planning Council, set up in 1964, made a study (published in 1967) in which the importance of the road network to the economy of the south west was explained and emphasised. Some of its conclusions were unremarkable, such as that resulting from an expensive and lengthy investigation, suggesting that building a bridge over the river Severn would change for the better the economic prospects of South Wales: this was a conclusion which I and other members of the Council had reached long before the production of a detailed study by our learned economist and statistician, Sam Edwards. Of greater interest was its evidence of the chronic overloading of the

A38 trunk road, which included the stretch from Bristol through Taunton to Exeter. The road was described as 'single two-lane carriageways ... of sub-standard width and alignment ... carrying volumes of traffic at peak times much beyond their capacity, conditions being very bad at many points ... The congestion ... hinders the normal commercial traffic of the region.' When you consider the make-up of the Economic Planning Councils, their members being appointed by a Labour government, those were strong words. Such emphasis was justified: the dual carriageway which was constructed in 1957 along the stretch of highway less than a mile in length from Walford Cross to Monkton Elm was at the time the longest on the entire A38 trunk road in Somerset.

In 1961 the railway had opened a Coal Concentration Depot in Taunton to counter the trade it was losing in coal and anthracite from Wales through Bridgwater Docks and from the Midlands by road. A condition of using the depot was that the merchant was not permitted to use road transport other than for local delivery. The biggest coal distributor, Goodlands, whom we have met before, stayed with the scheme until it was wound up a few years later, after which the railway virtually conceded defeat so far as the haulage of goods was concerned. The Beeching report had been published in 1963 and there was little for the Planning Council to record except that, apart from the main lines from Taunton to Bristol, Exeter and Westbury, there was no possibility of putting back the clock so far as the carriage of freight by rail was concerned.

The Planning Council also examined passenger transport by road and painted a desolate picture of a loss-making bus industry providing a poor and unreliable service. This situation was inevitable with the (driver-and-conductor) double-manning, lack of investment, union control, indifferent management and political intermeddling inherent in any nationalised undertaking. The industry was descending in the familiar downward spiral, where bad service led to fewer customers which led to bigger losses which led to lower investment which led to poorer equipment and to poorer pay which led to shortages of staff which led to bad service. The government then put up the prices to stem the losses, losing still more customers and accelerating the descent. You also had to take into account the stringencies of the Public Sector Borrowing Requirement, whereby the Treasury gobbled up any spare cash, including that generated by a depreciation of assets, but blocked investment. The nationalised water authorities were to suffer in the same way, with a further twist that successive governments wanted any tariff rises to be concentrated on industry (which had no votes) but not on members of the public (who could vote).

(I knew all about the water dilemma as an insider, being a member of the Wessex Water Authority from 1979. I was surprised to learn some time afterwards that the Secretary of State (Lord) Roy Hattersley had personally intervened to try to block my appointment. Politicians distrust those who wear no political labels. The Conservatives were more successful in vetoing my appointment to the South Western Electricity Board against the recommendation of the Chairman and his colleagues.)

Another government committee was set up in 1967 to study what were called 'The Intermediate Areas' under the chairmanship of Sir Joseph Hunt, its membership again being appointed by the Labour government with its mandatory quota of trade union officials and academics. Sir Joseph was himself a manufacturer, as were two other members, and they received unexpected support from two other of the nine who unexpectedly 'crossed the floor' during the committee's deliberations. In the teeth of 'advice' freely and continuously offered by the distinguished assessors from the Civil Service who sat with them, including Mr. Pugh whom we have already met, the majority of the Committee recommended in 1969 that industrial growth would best be stimulated by 'a transition from financial policies based on incentives to policies of strengthening the infrastructure'. In particular 'a high degree of priority should be given to the completion of a "spine" road from Bristol to Plymouth'.

This was not what the government or the bureaucrats wanted to hear. It also proved too much for an academic member, a distinguished Professor of Economics, Arthur Brown, who, having no industrial experience himself, persisted in the view that you can create wealth in a poor area by penalising growth in a rich one, declaring that there was 'no warrant here for a switch of emphasis to infrastructure investment'. His Note of Dissent, including the proposal of a 'congestion tax' on all employees in prosperous areas, remains a classic exposition of how not to take advantage of the energy and enterprise of individuals in the creation of wealth and employment.

Relief for the motorist and haulier was, however, at hand. It would of course have been unworthy of the British to copy Hitler's *Autobahnen* before 1939, although, as we have noted, the Kingston bypass did use some of the same ideas. With the war won, the first tentative stretches of motorway were planned, usually too narrow, always too late. The Preston bypass was built and, looking west, two narrow lanes were provided from Brentford to Maidenhead and two more, equally narrow, from Tewkesbury to Halesowen. Controversy about how best to work your way through the congested cities of Birmingham or Bristol and take advantage of the available strips of motorway threatened for a time to supplant sex and soccer as a topic of male conversation in the bar of any licensed premises. Bit by bit odd ribbons of motorway appeared in the south west: from Clevedon to Edithmead and bypassing Collumpton. A bridge carrying the M5 over the Avon near Bristol had been planned for completion by 1971 but became the subject of interminable guerrilla warfare between unions and management which seemed unlikely to result in victory for either. Even when the motorway was completed, traffic for London from Taunton took the GWR—the 'Great Way Round'—or struggled though lanes and villages to save 17 miles by picking up the A303 near Sparkford.

Taunton too was changing. West Country Building Societies, which had operated out of accountants' or solicitors' offices, acquired their own premises on the main streets, soon to be joined by their national competitors. Banks bought up adjacent shops to double and re-double their frontages. Lloyds destroyed much of the façade of Georgian Hammet Street with a modern building. Barclays caused the closure of the only bar in town which, serving all its ales directly from the wood, defied the pressure of the brewers to supply gassy keg beer or nothing. Family businesses were taken over, to be renamed as part of a chain of stores or closed. Multiples changed the face of the main shopping streets by imposing their corporate fascias. There were a few muted objections to the destruction of what had survived the war but money talks, and the banks and building societies and property companies had loud voices, smooth lawyers and long purses.

A further development, which was to have far-reaching effects on the transport and distribution industry, was the emergence of the supermarkets, first in the town centre and then on the periphery. The days when every supplier made individual deliveries to each retailer had long vanished. Much of the local distribution went through the warehouses of wholesale grocers who took in bulk supplies from many suppliers and made single deliveries to retailers. There were also the buying consortia like Mace, Londis and Spar who stored goods centrally. These wholesalers served small retailer, town-centre store or corner shop alike. There had been multiples too, like Liptons, the Co-ops and Sainsbury's, operating out of the main shopping streets and concentrating on the sale of groceries and provisions. They too used their own depots to consolidate onward deliveries into the retail outlets.

All this changed when the town-centre multiple store became a supermarket and then when the supermarkets relocated either in town with a dedicated car park or out of town altogether. Over the years more and more food and drink was channelled through the Regional Distribution Centres of the supermarket chains, with small traders losing business to their powerful rivals. As food retailing became more sophisticated, so too did the supporting services of warehousing and transport, threatening to eliminate both the small producer and the local haulier, along with the corner shop.

Another revolution arrived with the development of Information Technology. Whereas in the old days staff in a retail store might check the shelves weekly to see what had been sold and then order replacement stock, the introduction of Electronic Point of Sale (EPOS) equipment and bar-coding allowed a central inventory controller to re-order each evening what had been sold that day in all the outlets, in the knowledge that the shortages would be delivered to his main depots within 36 hours. As a further refinement, the re-ordering could by-pass the manufacturer and go direct to a haulier who held a buffer stock in a warehouse on the manufacturer's behalf, under contract to deliver it to any supply depot in the United Kingdom within 24 hours of receiving instructions. The supermarkets also accelerated the trend towards the sale of chilled foods, which are more difficult to keep fresh than frozen foods or dry goods (such as soap powder or sultanas) and have to be rotated accurately and turned over quickly. Along with the practice of chilling came the 'sell by' gimmick, which especially applies to chilled foodstuffs and drinks, requiring complex inventory rotation in the warehouse to ensure that everything delivered has the requisite shelf life.

Taunton was changing, the retail trade was changing, and life for a haulier was becoming more and more complicated. The simpler world which Tom Hewett and Ken Thorne had known was being threatened by the computer, the mobile phone, the supermarket, the motorway, the 'sell-by' date, the Regional Distribution Centre, consolidation, shared-user. Even if the day of the privately-owned local haulage business was not coming to an end, its life was going to become increasingly difficult. It is not surprising that so many owners, like Philip Langdon, had decided to get out while the going was not too rough and before the increasing capital cost of staying in the business would have to be met out of their own wallets.

Twelve

How Langdons Changed Ownership and Location

As we saw, the first negotiation for the sale of Tone Vale Transport, Taunton Meat Haulage and West Somerset Warehousing in 1974 (which for brevity we will in future lump together as Langdons) was with a firm in Southampton. Whether this was Solent Shipping and Transport, with which Langdons was to co-operate for some years and of which Ken Thorne became a director, is uncertain. Before the talking with potential buyers started, Philip Langdon explained to Tom Hewett that a purchaser of the business would want to deal with a single person. Tom thereupon transferred to Philip his shares in Taunton Meat Haulage, thus eliminating the only minority shareholding.

When the Southampton talks led to nothing, the company's insurance brokers, Price and Pierce, one of the then fashionable conglomerates, came forward as a buyer and a deal was struck with them. As was usual with many businesses in those days, and especially family-owned ones, the staff had no service agreements and their limited perks included insurance against death or sickness in service, but no pension. As a buyer would want to ensure continuity of management, contracts of service for a period of five years were signed, certainly by Tom Hewett and Ken Thorne and possibly by two or three others, with a non-competition clause of two years tying them to the new owner. Philip Langdon was to remain Managing Director. There was nothing unusual or sinister in any of this because the goodwill of the business depended on Tom and Ken, and on Philip himself.

It is easy for us to forget how few smaller firms offered pension schemes for their employees even in the 1970s, although some enlightened employers realised that failure to do so could prove a false economy. Certainly the success of Avimo after 1960 was founded on the quality of its staff, and the calibre of those it attracted, based on equal perks for all, including contributory pensions (but no company cars, even for the Managing Director). In those days, when a smaller firm without a pension scheme was taken over by a company which had one, the new employees usually had to join the scheme: and they sometimes also received retrospective credit for their years of employment before the acquisition. In the latter case the cost of funding prior service normally had to be found by the seller or deducted from the purchase price, which amounts to the same thing.

Because the Langdon companies had no pension scheme, it would have cost someone, Philip Langdon in this instance, around £30,000 to top up the Price and Pierce pension fund to cover just the prior service of the senior managers. This was a considerable sum at that time, and so it was not done. Philip's understandable failure to do so was to remain a source of discontent for Tom Hewett and Ken Thorne, and especially after their retirement. In these days of portable pensions, the vendor of a private business is not faced with this dilemma and old servants can expect better protection. But we must beware judging what happened a quarter of a century ago by the standards of today.

On the face of it, Price and Pierce should have been a good fit with Langdons. It already had another business in Taunton which manufactured paper-making machinery. More significantly, it was the owner of three other road-transport businesses in the United Kingdom and two more in France. However its management seems to have made no effort, then or after it in turn had been taken over, to integrate Langdons into a wider grouping, either to achieve economies of scale or to make use of the national and European distribution coverage which, in theory at least, should have been achievable.

The reality was that Price and Pierce owned a collection of companies which, outside transportation, had little in common. It was in timber and woodpulp, with significant involvement in Holland and the Middle East. It had travel agencies and interests in overseas property. It was in the horticultural business and, as we saw, it was an insurance broker. If you read the Annual Report for 1977 of Tozer Kemsley and Millbourn, after TKM had taken over the company, you might infer that the only valuable thing about TKM's victim was the lease of Price and Pierce's London Head Office.

Langdons also had a mention in that Report: 'Langdon showed improvement'. Faint praise indeed! But the reference to Langdons in the Annual Report for the year 1976 had not been very encouraging either: 'Reduced capital use, stringent controls on credit and on day to day expenditure resulted in reduced interest costs and a welcome return to profitability', from which we must infer that, in its first year under Price and Pierce, Langdons had made a loss.

When TKM bought Price and Pierce, and so also Langdons, it was riding high with profits stemming in large measure from the valuable concession for the sale of BMW cars in the United Kingdom. (It is bizarre to recall that BMW started its life in car manufacture as a licensee for building the Longbridge Austin 7.) Like Price and Pierce, TKM was a conglomerate, a rag-bag of companies, and displayed a shaky Balance Sheet. So long as the cash from the BMW franchise rolled in, the structure looked solid. When the franchise was lost in 1980, the prop for the whole edifice was withdrawn and the rest of the rather ramshackle building started crumbling towards collapse.

The TKM Report and Accounts for 1981 made no specific mention of Langdons, but reported that 'the strengthening of Sterling had had a severe impact on the transport companies'. (Times change but Chairman-speak doesn't.) Wadham Stringer, the TKM subsidiary concerned with car distribution, had moved into loss. In 1982 Wadham Stringer returned to profit, albeit now reliant on the dubious privilege of selling the products of British Leyland. Transport had returned to profitability, it was said, although the adjectives 'disappointing' and 'difficult' told their own story. The next Report told shareholders that 'The Road Haulage Market remains extremely weak and although showing overall profitability the performance of these companies in 1983 was far from satisfactory. The current year (1984) has not started well and a drive to rationalise and reduce costs is being undertaken.' This was more Chairman-speak meaning 'things are in a mess'. Clearly the bad start was maintained because the Report on 1984 said that it had been a very poor year for the road-haulage interests both in the U.K. and in France. Not for the first time there was a note of optimism: 1985 had started better but the overall performance remained disappointing.

The vaguely optimistic Report for 1984 was dated 28 June 1985. Three days later, on 1 July, the cat finally leapt out of the bag. In a circular to all shareholders, the Chairman wrote: 'I became Chairman of Tozer in December 1982 at a time when the Group was in a precarious financial position and its future was in doubt. At that time

Tozer had an excessive level of borrowings, which had mainly arisen from an ambitious expansion programme. In addition the Group had incurred substantial trading and extraordinary losses which had significantly eroded shareholders' funds. At 31st December, 1982 Group net borrowings were £103 million compared with shareholders' funds at the same date of £15 million.' In effect, since the loss of the BMW franchise, the business had drifted towards insolvency. Only an injection of new equity capital from a company controlled by the New Zealand industrialist and financier, (Sir) Ron Brierley, was to save TKM from receivership, and control passed to Brierley.

A sad story, you will agree, but relevant in the Langdons' context because these two conglomerates, Price and Pierce and then TKM, were its parent companies from 1974 to 1986. I have given a brief résumé of their descent into the pit so that, so far as Langdons was concerned, we can divide those years into four periods. There was the brief ownership by Price and Pierce; then four years or so under TKM, when expansion seemed possible and the parent company was not short of cash. The period 1980 to 1984 was one of growing hardship: instead of a subsidiary being able to call on the parent for funding, the parent needed every penny it could extract from the subsidiary, whether through profits, asset sales or simply persuading a local banker to increase its overdraft facilities. Then, after the Brierley rescue, the decision came either to close or sell the transport companies. As we look at what was happening with Langdons during these years, we must bear in mind in which of these four time zones its parent was operating.

Not a lot changed for Langdons, it seems, under the brief Price and Pierce ownership apart from the introduction of the owner-driver scheme, which we have already noted, and the move to Norton Fitzwarren. Before its troubles started in 1980, TKM took a more positive view of Langdons and developed a sensible strategy of moving into combined warehousing and haulage instead of just providing a set of wheels in competition with every other licensed operator or cowboy in the business. There is a saying in the hairdressing trade that you should always 'wet the customer's head': once she (mainly) has wet hair, she cannot get up and leave if the staff are too busy to attend to her. So it is with warehousing. Anyone can quote on a 'spot' basis for carrying goods from A to B. If however the haulier is also warehousing the customer's stock, it is more difficult for the customer to use a third party for inward and outward transport, and likely to lead to inefficiency because, to put it mildly, the third party is not going to receive preferential service when he visits a store run by a competitor. You also introduce another handling process, in which mistakes can be made for which it will be hard to pin down liability. We will observe this phenomenon more closely when we return to Taunton Cider.

During phase two, the good years under TKM, Tone Vale Transport continued to work for the Wansborough Paper Company in Watchet for whom it stored two- or three-ton reels of paper in addition to doing some of the onward transport. Through the introduction of a Bristolian called Douglas Ramsay, a deal was struck with the Finnish Paper Company, later renamed Varma, to collect their reels of paper from the London docks, either shipped in containers or individually, and store them for onward distribution. To house this stock and have other space available, Langdons took the lease for 25 years on two newly-built warehouses at Arnos Castle in Bristol. One of them, Arnos B, had a high roof and a strengthened floor, allowing the reels of paper to be stacked on top of each other to what always looked a precarious extent.

The principle of combining storage with distribution applies just as much to the temperature-controlled side of the business as it does to the ambient. To capture some of the considerable traffic in chilled and frozen food passing through the port of Avonmouth, TKM allowed Langdons to convert the smaller warehouse, Arnos C, from ambient to temperature-controlled. The long and expensive business of insulating the store and installing the refrigeration equipment was put in hand, financed by a loan of £150,000 from another TKM subsidiary which dealt in hire-purchase. There was also talk in addition of a major distribution contract for Birds Eye Wall's, which evaporated when TKM were unable to fund the necessary temperature-controlled facilities.

With the two warehouses under lease, Douglas Ramsay joined the firm as manager of the Arnos Castle operation, and yet another company was formed within the Langdons' sub-group to run the business. In addition to the Varma paper, a motley range of dry goods was stored in Arnos B and, for a time, Langdons had no trouble in finding other business for the refrigerated storage space at Arnos C: indeed in 1983 it took on the lease of another cold store in nearby Whitby Road to cope with the excess. Yet the main object of converting Arnos C had not been achieved. Because the firm still sold only refrigerated space, it failed to achieve the intended vertical integration, which left the transport side offering no more of a service than any Tom, Dick or Harry who had a tractor and a refrigerated box. As we will discover in due time, the legacy of the leases of the properties at Arnos Castle and Whitby Road was to haunt the company in years to come.

We have seen how Taunton Meat Haulage and West Somerset Warehousing found their different ways to the old SRD at Norton Fitzwarren. In 1979 TKM, still in its palmier days, agreed that Langdons could buy a freehold site on which all its Taunton-based operations could be brought together. There were two candidates, an old military complex in Bindon Road, Taunton, where the firm rented some space; or a site of six and a half acres four miles from Taunton in the direction of Bridgwater on the A38 at Walford Cross, with a warehouse built in 1940 for the storage of sugar and a pair of houses for the staff. Walford Cross was chosen but sadly TKM turned down the offer to include the two houses. This was to cause some restriction and expense when the environmental laws were changed, as we will discover in due course.

Langdons moved to Walford Cross in March 1981. The maintenance garage for Tone Vale Transport in Wiveliscombe was closed, and the premises in Ford Road were sold. Besides Walford Cross, the company still operated a dedicated store for ICI fertilisers in the SRD at Norton Fitzwarren and its leased premises at Arnos Castle, giving it about 250,000 cubic feet of temperature-controlled space and 150,000 square feet of dry storage. It also rented a two-man depot in west London on 1.3 acres, charged with obtaining return loads to the West Country. Philip Langdon, now Chairman, said at the time, 'We are very proud of the fact that we are still trading profitably, and more important, have not had to lay anybody off in spite of the drastic effect that the current recession has had on the storage and distribution industry.' More Chairman-speak, I fear: *plus ça change*! The firm by then operated 150 trailers, of which a third were temperature-controlled, although it was silent about how many it owned and how many were hired. It also used 60 drivers, apart from those on yard or 'shunter' vehicles, only two of whom were company employees. The other 58 tractors belonged to the owner-drivers. And from then on, day after day, week after week, every penny it scraped together or managed to borrow from the Midland Bank in Taunton would be extracted by TKM.

The customer list in 1980 is instructive, for those who have stayed the course this far, because it reveals that, apart from ICI and Varma, the fundamental issue of co-ordinating transport with storage had not been resolved:

1. Aaronson, a plasterboard manufacturer in South Molton, halfway from Taunton to Barnstaple. Ambient haulage only. 'Shunter' on customer's premises with Langdons' driver. Bad location for return loads with consequent excessive running 'light'. 'Spot' traffic only (meaning that an agreed rate per trip was paid but with no permanent contract).

2. TKM Foods, Spalding, a joint venture and then merger between TKM and HP Foods. Canned food and fresh fruit and vegetables under the brand name Smedleys, and chilled salads. A bonus from being part of TKM but no storage.

3. ICI. A good contract with inward haulage of fertiliser from Avonmouth and Immingham to Norton Fitzwarren, storage, and then onward delivery to wholesalers and farms.

4. Finnish Paper (Varma), as explained earlier, in Arnos B. Haulage from London to Bristol and then general delivery. Another solid contract.

5. The Intervention Board (government). Storage only of milk powder but at good rates because civil servants aren't spending their own money.

6. Lloyd Maunder, whom we have met before, but now way down the list. Transport only of chilled meat.

7. Anchor Butter coming into Avonmouth from New Zealand but now needing temperature-controlled vehicles. Not much storage.

8. Wincanton Transport, a much larger competitor, but you need to work with your competitors for return loads, and they with you.

It looked a more solid base for the business than it really was, and didn't change much in the next five years. The twin weaknesses were that many customers, including Aaronson, the biggest, were for haulage only, which meant that they could in theory take their business away at a day's notice, although providing a 'shunter'—an old unplated tractor to move trailers around in the customer's yard—gave some security: and, the other weakness, that so much of the warehousing was rented. It would become increasingly evident that the only consistently profitable storage activity was that at the freehold Walford Cross site. Elsewhere rent and rates increases over time eroded profit, and then turned profit into loss.

In 1980, Philip Langdon was thinking about retirement. Although both Ken Thorne and the Financial Director, Roy Hutchings, may have been considered, or considered themselves, as his successor, TKM decided to look elsewhere and appoint a Managing Director from outside the company or the Group. So it was that, in October 1980, Michael Donoghue, of whom we will hear much more, became Managing Director of Langdons in October 1980, with Philip staying on as Chairman. The business might understandably have suffered from a lack of drive after Philip Langdon had sold out to Price and Pierce: what motivates the donkey when it has eaten the carrot? Now there was the further complication: how to pass over the driving when you have been used for so long to sitting at the wheel yourself? Never an easy thing to do, especially when the company proudly bears your own name.

Thirteen

HOW DRINKING HABITS CHANGED AND TAUNTON CIDER CHANGED WITH THEM

Our last look at Taunton Cider was in 1971 when Guinness joined other brewers in the consortium as a shareholder. Guinness was different. It brought to the party, cash aside, no string of tied outlets for the Taunton product but an unrivalled and unique expertise in marketing alcoholic drinks through third parties. Without owning pubs, it had, from its Dublin base, persuaded the world to buy the stout which it brewed, even though latterly it had been forbidden to claim that it was Good for You (although I am sure it must be). With *Harp*, it had also made deep inroads into the lager market.

The policy of accepting brewers into the Taunton consortium and then selling through their outlets had worked well, effectively absorbing all its available capacity for bottled and then draught cider. A consequence was that, prior to the arrival of Guinness, the firm was only selling significantly to that portion of the trade which was controlled by its shareholders, through the pubs which they ran under managers or which they leased to tenants. Nationally, sales through these two channels represented only 26 per cent of cider sales overall. Another 20 per cent went through 'free' pubs (if you know what I mean—I've never been lucky enough to discover one personally). Off-licences sold 9 per cent and other retailers like grocers and supermarkets took a staggering 45 per cent. If Taunton Cider wanted to expand its market share, it would have to find acceptability in the 74 per cent of the trade which it was not effectively addressing.

The volume of cider being drunk was also rising, despite the imposition of excise duty after 1984. Whereas most cider was sold in the 1960s and 1970s in bottles and flagons, with draught limited to the West Country in the form of traditional rough cider or scrumpy, in the 1980s the breakthrough was made into selling branded draught cider in pubs nationally. As a result the national output of 33 million gallons in 1970 rose to 91 million by 1991. Just by maintaining market share, a producer could expect to double its volume over the two decades. By the end of the 1980s, sales in pub bars were predominantly of draught cider, averaging 77 per cent of the total, and those through other channels obviously had to be in bottles or cans—'packaged' as it is called in the business. Despite the introduction of draught sales through pubs, taken overall there remained in the market as a whole a predominance of packaged sales, which by 1991 had grown in volume to be half again greater than draught.

Another development was the splitting of the market into three segments which could be described as regular brands, special brands and own labels: the trade tended to call them 'Mainstream', 'Premium' and 'Retail'. The mainstream brands were ordinary cider, competitively priced, such as Taunton's *Autumn Gold*, which as we saw came as a bonus with the acquisition of the Quantock Vale Cider Company. The premium brands were those which had fancy packaging, possibly a higher alcoholic content, and certainly a lot more spent on advertising, of which Taunton's *Diamond White* and *Blackthorn* are examples. Then there are the retail brands or 'own-label' sales, increasingly through supermarkets, where the same product might be marketed under different names. Although those of us who are not connoisseurs of cider might suppose that there would not be much difference in the profitability of each of these product types after the cost of promotion was taken into account, we would be wrong. In 1992, for example, the regular or 'mainstream' brands took 53 per cent of the market by volume and 44 per cent by value; the special or 'premium' brands took 26 per cent by volume and 39 per cent by value; and the own-label or 'retail' production was 21 per cent by volume and 17 per cent by value. It did not require a financial genius to work out that the special brands were very good news and the own-label business not so hot.

The nightmare of any national cider producer was that the product would turn into just another commodity, that a customer might walk into a pub or shop and ask for no more than sweet or dry cider. The truth is that Polish apple juice is no different from that grown in Somerset, albeit much cheaper, and there is no shortage in Belgium of chemists who can replicate the taste of any branded cider and produce it there without the overhead of launching and protecting brands.

Despite the lower margins, there are advantages in manufacturing products which someone else has to market and sell. The business provides bulk sales to a limited number of customers on a regular basis without the overhead of advertising and other promotional costs, and with distribution by the lorry-load rather than in individual cases, pallets or barrels. The downside is first that the price is going to be very keen and constantly under competitive pressure; secondly, under an own-label deal the manufacturer retains no goodwill in the brand; and thirdly, the retailer will expect the same quality of service as he gets from all his other suppliers. That is where distribution comes in and we will be coming back to this last point in some detail as our tale unfolds.

The acquisition of Quantock Vale brought a major bonus to Taunton. The cider makers at Quantock Vale had shown great ingenuity in developing and producing new variants. In addition to copying *Autumn Gold*, they produced a dry white cider which was made, originally, from Bramley apples. It was dressed up in large bottles rather like champagne and sold under the name *Pommia*: not an arresting title, we might suppose, but slightly more up-market then the English translation of the phonetic French 'apple tree'. *Pommia* didn't sell particularly well under that name, nor was it immediately successful when it was re-packaged in half-pint non-returnable green bottles and re-christened *Diamond White*. This repackaging was in itself a daring innovation, because the concept of using disposable glass bottles was new in the mid-80s. The trade was so used to returning empties to the bottler in crates that many doubted whether the publican would adjust easily to throwing glass bottles away, and, if he did, whether the dustman would accept them.

Miles Roberts, then Taunton's Managing Director, learned on a trip to the Scottish sales office nestling at Queensferry under the abutments of the Forth Bridge that the Caledonian market liked *Diamond White*, and that it was in short supply. At that time, because of its poor sales, the brand was about to be phased out. On his return to Norton Fitzwarren, it was agreed to give the Scots a £60,000 promotion budget for three months to see if they could develop *Diamond White* sales. At much the same time Martin Warby, who held a senior position in Sales, agreed with Bass for them to stock *Diamond White* in some of their Midland pubs.

There is a saying in the brewing industry that you can never sell a beer north of where it is brewed, which, if true, would be bad news for Palmers in Bridport and

Eldridge, Pope in Dorchester, among others. It is right, however, to observe that what sells in Scotland or the Midlands is likely to find general acceptance through the rest of the United Kingdom. The effect of £60,000 worth of free *Diamond White* on Scottish taste-buds was sensational. The stocking by Bass went equally well and the rest, as they say, is history. Taunton Cider had its premium brand, which Peter Marney, then Taunton's chief cider maker, had been able to produce using the concentrate of European culinary varieties of apple, or what we laymen would call cooking apples, after which volume production was no longer constrained by having to stay with Bramleys.

When Guinness came aboard in 1972, the marketing focus was changed in line with their own methods of selling stout and lager beers. In addition to our old friends *Natch* (a contraction of its former name *Natural Dry*), *Diamond White* and *Autumn Gold*, the company introduced in 1972 the draught cider which they called *Dry Blackthorn*. There were other brands too, but these were the ones which took off, along with *Red Rock*, another special brand which was launched later, although without so much success. Guinness remained a shareholder until 1985, during which time it provided as its Taunton Cider director an experienced marketing man and taught the company a thing or two about brand development. It also received a special fee for marketing advice, which, when it reached £1 million a year, grated with the other brewer-shareholders who felt that their contribution in this regard was not without its value.

To support the brands, Taunton Cider set up specialist sales and marketing teams for the various sectors of its business, and by 1992 no less than 12 per cent of the company's turnover was being spent on advertising and other promotional activities and a third of the entire staff was involved one way or another in sales and marketing.

The departure of Guinness from the consortium in no way changed the marketing policy by then adopted at Norton Fitzwarren. In 1983 Peter Adams was appointed Marketing Director. Although still a young man, he had gained useful experience in brand development and management with ICI, Spillers, and Heinz before becoming managing director of a toy manufacturer. Dog food, children's toys and pharmaceutical products may not seem particularly cognate with alcoholic drinks, but the trick with all marketing is to have a product which a customer wants to buy in preference to whatever else is available at the right time for a price which he or she will pay, even if there is no real need for it. In 1987 Mr. Adams was appointed Managing Director and, when Miles Roberts retired from his position as Executive Chairman in 1990 (after 23 years in charge), he became a forceful Chief Executive with a full appreciation of the value of brand equity and how it should be exploited.

As the business grew, so the proportion of local apples used to make the cider had to fall, finally representing no more than 10 per cent of the cider produced. In 1992 the firm had contracts to take the crop from 800 acres of orchards in Somerset and Devon, as well as owning 40 acres of its own, but beyond that there were few British apples available. Concentrated apple juice from the continent, especially from Italy and Germany, was however both cheaper and more reliable as a source than what came from good old English orchards, where a late frost could play havoc with the yield. Taunton Cider still came up from Somerset, but not much of it from cider apples grown there.

As those who have reached this far may have gathered, in any business distribution is as much a part of the process of production as making the stuff in the first place. Because a substantial amount of its sales went to Scotland, Taunton Cider for many years shipped by rail direct from the siding into its site in Norton Fitzwarren. The channel worked well and the firm wanted to extend the concept to include outward delivery to Yorkshire as well as the import of apple juice from Italy. British Rail, who might have been expected to enthuse about this traffic, withdrew its *Speedlink* service as privatisation approached. Two private companies, Tiger Rail and Charterail, tried to take on the service but both ended up in receivership. Thereafter all transport, both inward and outward, had to be carried by road, being trunked to depots from which collections were made by customers, or delivered direct to retail customer stores and especially those of supermarkets. The loss of the rail link to Scotland after January 1993 led to an increase in road traffic of four or five loads a day.

The drinks trade is cyclical, with people being thirstier in the summer (usually) than in winter (other than at Christmas and New Year). In the old days, before sell-by dates and all that kind of thing, Brian Longstaff, the able and highly respected Director of Operations at Norton Fitzwarren, was able to run his plant at an even and efficient rate throughout the year, storing much of the winter production for sale in the summer. The insistence of retailers and others for date-stamping, however irrelevant it may be to public health, led to a reduced demand for outside storage and a more lumpy production. The factory became less efficient as it moved from 'make for stock' to 'make to order' and the position may have been exacerbated rather than eased by the plethora of consultants who were retained at great cost by the company, with their bright ideas and buzz words and phrases, among which 'supply-chain management' became a favourite. It means trying to make what customers want when they want it without building inventory and, thanks to the spreadsheet, accountants are able to show sensational reductions in working capital if it is introduced. The downside is that the customer often doesn't know what he will want until the day before, by when it is too late to make it, whereupon he will buy it from a competitor.

By 1990 Taunton Cider operated a fleet of 16 38-tonne articulated units (curtain-siders), topping it up with spot hire at peak times. However the bulk of its traffic was carried on spot rates by outside hauliers. Langdons started working for Taunton Cider in 1986, when their annual billing for haulage amounted to £99,368. We will be looking closely at what happened between Langdons and Taunton Cider later on; at this stage all we should note is that the traffic billed by Langdons had grown to £1,255,441 by 1995, and represented a large part of its ambient, or not temperature-controlled, haulage business.

In the late 1980s, due in large measure to greater advertising and rising prosperity, sales of bottled and canned cider grew more rapidly than those of draught. Bulmers in Hereford was never a firm to sit back and watch a rival eat into its market, and competition in the draught side of the business actually led to a fall in Taunton's share between 1987 and 1991. It is also possible that inter-company talks between the big three, Bulmers, Taunton Cider and Showerings, which of course were confined to discussion of technical matters and would never have broken the law by touching upon pricing policies or market shares, became less frequent and cordial than had at one time been the case.

Another factor affecting the market arose after 1990 when the Monopolies and Mergers Commission ordered the larger brewers to divest themselves of substantial numbers of tied houses. In 1991 60 per cent of Taunton's output went to pubs, and 42 per cent of what went to pubs went to three companies, Bass, Courage, and Scottish and Newcastle. Although five-year non-exclusive supply agreements were signed with two of the trio, the freer trading environment was a mixed blessing: it could prove an advantage if Taunton managed to get better terms from smaller groups with less purchasing power, or a problem, when what had hitherto been a closed market was opened up to competitors. There was a further complication when Courage was itself acquired by Grand Metropolitan, who had previously placed an exclusive contract with Bulmers.

Then there was the emergence of alcoholic lemonades and so on, the dreaded 'alcopops'.

Financially by the end of the 1980s Taunton Cider was going splendidly, as the following figures show for the years to 30 April:

	1988	1989	1990	1991
£m				
Turnover	57.5	59.5	77.7	109.4
Profit before interest and tax	4.8	5.3	8.2	10.5

There were, however, some niggling issues between the management and the brewer/shareholders. The first related to management incentives, the second stemmed from the possible threat to the sale of beer from an increase in cider drinking, and the third was resentment over the size of the special fee which Guinness had been paid, although alone among the shareholders Guinness had not benefited from special discounts for the cider, because it sold none.

You can take two views of management incentives. The old guard, among which Miles Roberts might have been included for all his innovation and dynamism, tended to take the view that you pay managers a salary for doing a job and if they don't think it is enough, they should go and work for themselves or for someone else. The business belongs to its shareholders or owners, who provide the capital, suffer any losses and should be entitled to hang on to the profit. The contrary view, shared by many younger managers who may have observed with admiration or envy how these things are done in the United States, is that they should be entitled to share personally in any significant enhancement in the value of the company, additional to their salary and any other perks. Furthermore, to retain the services of high-fliers, these additional benefits have to be offered.

The younger managers made these points to Courage and Bass in particular, being the largest shareholders, and their suggestions were received with a certain sympathy. In the shareholders' view, perhaps, Taunton Cider was not much of a business compared with their own massive concerns, and they were not bothered if its managers received, as they themselves hoped to, rewards beyond what was stated in their contracts of employment. Yet nothing happened, perhaps because, with its unusual shareholder structure, introducing a management-incentive scheme presented a certain amount of complication compared with a more conventional firm and partly because Miles Roberts was not enthusiastic about the idea.

The competition point was not really significant, although some thought it was. The licensed trade was under attack, as it saw it, from the Monopolies and Mergers Commission but the increase in cider consumption was not generally seen to have been at the expense of beer sales. Even if it was, the products were not perceived as becoming competitors, especially among women and young men, who in pubs tended to drink lager. The reality was that the output of cider was and would continue to be constrained by the availability of its raw materials, apples and apple juice. And yet on the one hand Miles Roberts felt that the outside directors were dragging their feet when it came to authorising capital expenditure on plant needed in Norton Fitzwarren further to increase production (and so perhaps eat still more into their own sales of beer). On the other hand Brian Longstaff was not aware of any such withholding of capital approvals, provided they were prepared with full technical, marketing and financial justification.

Another irritant was the special financial treatment of Guinness which remained a sore point with Bass especially, even after Guinness had left the consortium, and was to colour the view taken by the owners when Guinness later bid for the Taunton Cider.

None of these issues on its own was enough to make the shareholders want to change the status quo but their combined effect was that, one way and another, Taunton Cider was perceived by its outside directors to be becoming something of a distraction, an irritant even, and the brewers who were its shareholders decided to put it up for sale.

Once Taunton Cider was in play, the owners received serious approaches from at least three potential buyers. One was Cinven, an investment company flush with pension funds; another was Guinness; and the third was a fast-growing company in the drinks trade called Matthew Clark plc, of which Peter Aikens, who had been a director of Taunton Cider while working for Courage, was now Managing Director. Mr. Aikens realised the potential of the cider market and was determined to add that drink to the others which Matthew Clark already produced or marketed. He was in 1992 to bring off a major coup when he bought Showerings from a buy-out team headed by John Wilkinson, which had previously acquired Showerings from Allied Breweries but not done well with it, possibly because it had paid too high a price. Taunton Cider had itself looked closely at buying Showerings, but not at the kind of figure the management buy-out team offered. With Showerings, Matthew Clark acquired the cider-makers Gaymers, Coates and Whiteways to join its existing drinks companies, Saccone and Speed, a 'British' sherry made in Leeds, and Stowells of Chelsea. None of the venerable cider brands—Gaymers, Coates, Whiteways, Showerings—had exploited their names with anything like the flair shown by Bulmers and Taunton Cider and *Babycham* no longer occupied the pole position on the starting grid when it came to female pub-drinking habits.

As we will see, the prospective buyers failed to make an acceptable offer for Taunton Cider and, in the end, Peter Adams led a successful management buy-out which was completed on 22 May 1991, an announcement being first made at the retirement party of Miles Roberts as Chairman.

At 30 April 1991 Taunton Cider employed 451 people. Of these 149 were engaged in sales and other commercial activities, which means that many of them would have been based away from Norton Fitzwarren. At a guess, some 400 employees were living in and around Taunton. There were also the peripheral jobs created by any successful manufacturing business, not just in firms like Langdons who provided a direct service to the company, but in all the other trades and activities which go towards making up our complex industrial consumer society—people working in shops, schools, the building trades, local government, banks, building societies, garages, restaurants: the list goes on and on, with perhaps three or four people in service jobs for every one in productive employment. The prosperity of a great many people and their families was linked to that of Taunton Cider and Brian Longstaff used to hold seminars at which local people could learn of the benefits to the entire community which flowed from having such a firm in their midst. A company is created out of the efforts of all the people who work in it. Miles Roberts, Brian Longstaff and Peter Adams had done a great job for their employees, for Norton Fitzwarren and for Taunton in building such a strong and successful operation. In 1939 Taunton Cider and Langdons had been much the same size. By 1991, one had proved to be a hare and the other a tortoise.

But we are getting ahead of ourselves again, and before looking at the buy-out, and what happened next, we must retrace our steps for a decade, to the time when Michael Donoghue joined Langdons.

Fourteen

HOW LANGDONS FOUND AN EXPERIENCED MANAGING DIRECTOR AND EMPLOYED A CONSULTANT

As we saw, Peter Adams's previous experience well qualified him for the job at Taunton Cider where success depended to a great extent on his expertise in the exploitation of its brands. Similarly Michael Donoghue's preparation for his appointment as Managing Director of Langdons in October 1980 could not have been more thorough. Some 32 summers previously he had been born the son of the proprietor of a large wholesale grocery distribution business in Edinburgh. When Booker, a national distribution company, had bought it, his father had become Managing Director of their Scottish operations. Michael had been put to work at the age of 16 in a wholesale grocery business and stayed in the industry in various jobs for the next 10 years. At one time he found himself managing a retail grocery shop in Southend and by 1970 he was in Sheffield as Manager of a big Vestey Cash-and-Carry operation. When in 1972 he arrived back to Vestey's a day late after a holiday in the United States, he was sacked.

If Michael had caught the right transatlantic flight, or the one he did catch had been on time, he might never have left Cash-and-Carry, which is at the receiving end of the distribution business. The career change came within a week of losing his job with Vestey's when he moved into cold-store management. In 1977 he applied for a bigger job, still managing a cold-store, with the Swedish-owned company Frigoscandia and was appointed to a job he hadn't applied for, as General Manager of its Transport Division. As a result of these moves around the industry, when he joined Langdons he had spent several years on the receiving end of the food distribution business before switching first to the storage side and then to road transport. He also saw from the inside how some efficient operators controlled their businesses in an industry which is particularly subject to theft, stock loss and damage, apart from occasional misconduct by drivers and other hazards which arise when employees are of necessity not working under close supervision.

It was a thorough, if unacademic, grounding for the job of Managing Director of a transport, storage and distribution firm. We must remember that, even though about a million people work in distribution in the United Kingdom, the study of logistics is not a discipline which our finest seats of learning think worthy of a degree course, if indeed they think of it at all. We must recognise that it is much more important that the output of social scientists should not in any way be jeopardised by introducing less cerebral activities into tertiary education and so polluting the halls of Academe.

Michael's initiation into Langdons was not easy. The able accountant, Roy Hutchings, who thought perhaps that he might have been Philip Langdon's successor, decided to leave. Tom Hewett at Taunton Meat Haulage and Ken Thorne at Tone Vale Transport had each been allowed to row his own boat, with the two sides of the company maintaining separate workshops at Norton Fitzwarren and in Wiveliscombe. To a newcomer Langdons appeared to operate under an atmosphere which the Church of England bishops call 'creative conflict', but which laymen might describe as inefficient non-cooperation and petty squabbling. Then there was the powerful figure of Philip

The Langdons' senior management in 1980: from left to right, Tom Hewett, Philip Langdon, Ken Thorne and a youthful Michael Donoghue.

himself, the former owner and still Chairman, who had kept the company in profit through difficult years and might reasonably have doubts about the introduction of changes by the successor he had himself chosen in a business in which he had spent all his working life and which he knew inside-out.

When Michael Donoghue arrived, the Head Office of Langdons was in the rather down-at-heel location of a shed numbered 13 at the SRD in Norton Fitzwarren. Philip sensibly used an office styled the Boardroom as his own working area and suggested that his new Managing Director might be located in a caravan parked inside the warehouse. A compromise was reached when it was decided to erect a dividing wall in the Boardroom and proprieties were further preserved by giving the Chairman two thirds of the space, even though it meant the wall ended up halfway across a window.

Petty irritations and accommodation problems apart, Michael Donoghue faced two major challenges in turning Langdons into a company which would make a reasonable return on its capital. The first was that it owned virtually none of its equipment. There are indeed two schools of thought about buying or renting equipment in the transport industry. On the one hand, you can hire vehicles and trailers, preserving your capital for business expansion and therefore expanding beyond what you might otherwise afford. To obtain good rates from the hirers, you have to commit yourself to keeping the equipment for anything between one and three years, which is fine so long as the economy holds up and you don't lose any major customer. There is however the constant risk that you will find yourself with tractors and trailers parked up, and no income out of which you can pay the hire charges.

On the other hand, when you buy the equipment (even on hire purchase) you have something to sell if business drops, you obtain useful tax allowances, and you carry on using the kit long after it has been paid for. The expense is initially greater because you have to pay at least 10 per cent deposit at the outset, but thereafter the monthly cost of renting and hiring is much the same. Hire-purchase is normally not available on second-hand trailers and trucks, which imposes a good discipline, because it stops you buying rubbish. The lead time on buying new equipment can be several weeks, whereas rented trucks and trailers are always readily available, but, under pressure, you can always top up the fleet on a short-term basis with spot hire or sub-contractors while you wait for delivery. The firm may grow faster if you hire equipment, but you sleep more soundly if you buy it. There can be one snag: the company has to be a good credit risk if you decide to take the hire-purchase route.

In 1980 Langdons owned some flat-bed trailers of uncertain age, a few old refrigerated trailers, a shunter, and two tractors. Everything else was hired, or belonged to the owner-drivers.

The second major weakness we have already noted. Only two of the customers, Varma for paper and ICI for fertiliser, offered business which included inward haulage, warehousing and then outward distribution. Everything else consisted either of the provision of 'wheels' (transport only) on a spot basis, or the renting of space. None of the customers, not even Varma and ICI, had any commitment to continue placing work with Langdons. Nor indeed had Langdons anything special to offer them because its fleet was suited for the carriage of bulk loads rather than for local distribution, and its warehouses were neither racked to take pallets, nor were they staffed to carry out the 'picking' (the selection of goods from bulk for individual delivery) which an integrated operation demands.

The need to update the equipment was pressing because the day of loading flat-bed trailers manually was giving way to the use of fork-lift trucks and palletised loads. The sheeting and tying down of goods on a flat-bed is inefficient and time-consuming. In the trade the 'flats' were increasingly being replaced by curtain-sided vehicles, of which the proprietary 'Tautliner' is perhaps best known. Of course, the load still had to be secured within the trailer, but all the paraphernalia and cost associated with roping and sheeting, and the risk of rain damage, could be avoided.

Another of Michael Donoghue's problems was that Tozer Kemsley and Millbourn (or TKM as we have been calling the company) was moving into the phase, after the loss of the BMW distributorship, when it had no cash. TKM did, however, allow him in 1981, before the shutters descended, to buy five temperature-controlled trailers to the current standard which permitted them to carry 18 pallets. As there was no money for buying curtain-sided ambient trailers as well, he decided to convert 10 of the flat-beds to curtain-siders. This was a decision with which Philip Langdon strongly disagreed and thereafter relations between them, which had not always been easy, became less so.

Langdons' move into temperature-controlled food distribution was not made until October 1983, when it bought out a firm called A.G. Maidment and Sons based at Tisbury, near Salisbury. It did not buy Maidment's yard but took on its 22 rigid vehicles and its drivers. To retain the local trade, a depot was opened up in Fareham under the management of Rupert Ryall, whom we will meet again. The acquisition was only sanctioned by TKM because the price was cheap, and the price was cheap because the Maidment fleet was old and unreliable, a mixture of Seddons, Fords, Atkinsons, Leyland Freighters and Clydesdales, with (to continue the animal imagery) a Mastiff also thrown in. Such variety may seem attractive but makes life difficult for the workshops when it comes to holding spares, and especially with a fleet which must have been eagerly looking forward to its retirement, or being put out to grass, before Langdons bought it. But at least Michael Donoghue had the makings of an integrated transport business for chilled and frozen foods.

As we saw earlier, Langdons received a leg-up from its owner when it opened a depot in Spalding in 1981 to handle the work of its sister TKM subsidiary, Smedleys. This was especially good business because it was obtained without having to quote

Walford Cross in 1984.

against a competitor and was therefore booked at favourable rates: well, favourable for Langdons anyway. But Langdons and Smedleys were children of the same parent and had to do what father told them.

The move into the freehold premises at Walford Cross, four miles outside Taunton, took place in March 1981. Langdons still kept the rented ICI warehouse at the SRD in Norton Fitzwarren, along with other storage space there as needed. It had its warehouses at Arnos Castle in Bristol, to be later augmented by the one in Whitby Road. It had the London depot getting return loads to the west country, another depot for return loads in Manchester and the rather larger operation supporting Smedleys in Spalding.

A casual outsider might have concluded that this was a well-balanced business in both ambient and temperature-controlled distribution, nation-wide in its scope, the subsidiary of a famous public company and destined for greatness. A closer look revealed that the shell had very little nut in it. The fleet was rented or decrepit; the Bristol leases were a potential liability; the customers had no commitment to the business; the stores were not equipped for picking and distribution: the depots were too geographically separated for ease of control; Smedleys only used Langdons because it was told to; and, until 1983, the management was not always pulling in the same direction. We can add to its woes by recalling that TKM itself was in deep financial trouble and, after Ron Brierley's rescue, only wanted to get its cash out of the business as best it could.

Of the three remaining operational Langdon directors when Michael Donoghue was appointed, Tom Hewett retired in August 1984. He had been and remained a straightforward, loyal transport man, with great experience in refrigerated food haulage. As we noted, Ken Thorne was also a director of Solent Shipping and Transport in Southampton, whose relationship with Langdons is not altogether clear except that it was never part of the Price and Pierce/TKM package. Solent had been managed by Jack Fassett and, after his death in 1982, Ken Thorne found himself obliged to spend part of his time in Southampton. Some of the Solent equipment had in the past been maintained by Langdons in Wiveliscombe, with appropriate work sheets being prepared of course. Michael Donoghue was not able to fathom the precise relationship, if any, between the two companies but he was determined that Thorne should give his whole attention to a firm which was paying his salary as a full-time employee, which was Langdons.

Before the matter was resolved, Ken Thorne suffered a long illness requiring his absence from work for some months. When he returned he was still unwell and Michael was surprised to learn from the local Volvo dealer that Ken had ordered 10 new tractors for Langdons, without mentioning the decision to his Managing Director. Fortunately he was able to cancel the order on the grounds of Ken's ill-health, and indeed there would have been no money to pay for the vehicles anyway. Thereupon Ken Thorne left Langdons.

After the curtain-sider conversion, relations between Philip Langdon and Michael Donoghue remained cool, even though it was Philip who had shown considerable prescience in selecting someone as experienced and able as Michael as his successor. It was perhaps tactless of Philip to use Michael's secretary, Sheila Burnett (who is now Langdons' Personnel Manager) to type the letters to TKM which detailed his opinions about his Managing Director's shortcomings. In the end TKM suggested it might be better if Philip kept away from Walford Cross and, as he had moved to South Devon in anticipation of his impending retirement in May 1983, this advice he graciously accepted.

Philip Langdon's final visit to the company was not a happy one. As soon as he was in total control, Michael had ordered Trevor Horton, who managed the workshops, that nobody, but nobody, was entitled to draw free fuel from the company's pumps. Philip, as you might expect of an owner and Chairman, had been used to saving the company's money, and perhaps his own, by filling his car on business journeys with the firm's fuel. When, soon after his retirement, he called in to replenish his tanks, Trevor Horton declined to accommodate him. We can sympathise with Philip if he saw this as unacceptable insubordination. Trevor had joined the firm of B.A.Langdon in 1964 as an apprentice of sixteen, worked in the Cider House and in Ford Road, and was as Wiveliscombe as they come. Philip at once went to Mike Donoghue's office to complain. Michael was placed in a dilemma. If he didn't overrule Trevor, he would upset Philip: if he did, he would not be supporting a conscientious member of his staff. When Michael told Philip that Trevor was doing no more than carry out company policy, Philip closed the door of his office with such emphasis that it required the subsequent attention of a carpenter. Philip did, however, have the last word. He took his car to the filling station in nearby Bathpool which he had once owned and where the firm still ran an account, to which he booked the fuel.

With the departure of Philip Langdon, the illness of Ken Thorne, and Tom Hewett nearing retirement, Langdons recruited as Operations Manager Rob Swindells, who was then a youngish man of 32. He too came from the background of a family business but, being the eldest of six children and with the business struggling, he could not afford to take up the university places which he had been offered. After working as a roundsman for a laundry and then for a baker, he decided to obtain the HGV (Heavy Goods Vehicle) Class 1 licence which is requisite for driving large commercial vehicles. He spent two years as a lorry driver, much of it in Europe, before taking a reduction of half in earnings to become a trainee traffic manager with a subsidiary of the Transport Development Group. By 1980 he was manager of a transport depot from which he was recruited by Langdons in January 1983. As with Michael Donoghue, he had had a comprehensive training for the task which awaited him, of more practical use perhaps than the degree in Geography to which he had once aspired.

When Rob Swindells came aboard, Langdons had been doing badly. In 1981 it lost £17,000, on top of which TKM extracted £45,000 for what it described as 'management fees'. The loss in 1982 was £49,000. Early in 1983 a sister company, Laser Transport, was bought from TKM by its management and Michael Donoghue approached his masters to see if a similar deal might be done with Langdons. The story of those and other negotiations is best left for later, when we can see the full picture of how a buy-out was finally achieved. Suffice it to say at this stage that Langdons, under its new management, was performing rather better. Unfortunately its parent company knew it, which led to their asking an unrealistic price. The first round of discussions went on until May and then petered out. Indeed 1983 turned out to be a good year, with the firm showing a profit of £60,000 without any management fees. Michael was told bluntly that one of the reasons his proposals had been turned down was because the company was doing so well. There's encouragement for you!

The year 1984 started badly, with a loss of £46,000 in the first 34 weeks before more management charges, although part of that figure was a non-trading item in respect of redundancy payments. Having rejected the bid from the management, TKM played the card which people keep up their sleeve for this kind of crisis. It retained a consultant to assess the future prospects of Langdons, and to advise on what needed doing to make it successful.

The consultant's report was delivered in October 1984. In the eight years since 1977, the average profit before tax had been £33,000 and although turnover had risen from £2 million annually to £6 million, profitability had fallen. The equipment was old and expensive to maintain. Leasing costs, hire-purchase payments and depreciation amounted to £180,000 a year but more cash had to be introduced if the recommended capital investment of £220,000 a year was to be incurred: (and £220,000 was a serious under-estimate, in view of all the catching up which was necessary). Additional to the problems we have examined earlier - old and unreliable vehicles, lack of racked storage, dispersed operations, and so on - the report drew attention to the cost of bank-rolling owner-drivers, and picking up the debts of those who failed: in 19 months to the date of the report, £47,700 advanced to owner-drivers had been written off. And yet, without the tractors owned and operated by the owner-drivers, there was no business.

As anyone who has been in commerce knows, it is comparatively simple to indicate what is wrong, less easy to suggest a remedy, and then much harder to put the advice into practice. Among other things, the report listed the abysmal level of gross profit margins earned in each section of the business. The gross profit margin, for those who don't know these things, is the difference between the selling price and the direct costs associated with the particular activity, before taking into account general overheads like administration expenses, audit fees, interest, bank charges, office salaries, depreciation and so on. On all Langdons' haulage operations, the average gross profit margin was under 10 per cent The dedicated storage for Varma and ICI had gross margins of around 15 per cent and the chilled storage at Arnos C over 40 per cent, but the overall margin of 11 per cent meant that, without a change of direction and a major capital injection, the business would continue to drift downhill before eventually folding.

The consultant didn't spell this out so baldly, unless you read between the lines. His suggestions were:

* More spending on capital equipment (which was fine if someone was willing to provide the cash: Langdons was not going to generate it).

* Owner-drivers should be replaced by sub-contractors, although he recognised that without owner-drivers the firm would not have survived thus far.

* Appoint a specialist salesman (a good suggestion).

* Get out of Arnos B, and find somewhere cheaper. (He didn't mention this would depend on finding someone to take over an onerous lease.)

* Develop the contract hire side of the business, which he recognised would need still more capital injection. (He had mistakenly assumed that the business with Smedleys was on a contract hire basis. Contract hire—supplying dedicated at a fixed rate vehicles which are operated by the customer—is a game which only the big boys can play. It needs reliable equipment, immediately available replacements, and a nationwide repair service if it is to be run effectively. To suggest that Langdons was in any position to develop this business was unrealistic. The consultant also failed to report that, because of the firm's inability to replace equipment, the existing Smedleys contract was at risk.)

* In the medium term, relocate the business from Taunton to Exeter or Bristol where there would be more local business (although also more local competition).

He mentioned as the firm's strengths a simple management structure and good accounting procedures. The solutions, even when not fanciful, involved putting cash into the business, and that was something TKM, under Ron Brierley, was not prepared to contemplate. Having thought for a while of keeping Langdons, once it had digested the report TKM finally decided that there was no realistic alternative to selling the firm, along with its remaining transport operations.

TKM had by now deputed someone to sell its surplus businesses. My record of a discussion I had with him on 14 January 1985 about what the firm was worth recorded that 'he was not only unhelpful but plain rude.' I expect his note, if he made one, might have said the same thing in reverse. Having rejected the management proposal out-of-hand, he persuaded three or four competitors to take a look at Langdons, or at bits of it, such as the warehouse at Arnos C which was making money. When they found out some of the things to which you are now privy, they shook their heads and walked away. As hopes of a sale receded, Michael Donoghue faced the stark reality that either the firm would be closed or he would have to arrange a management buy-out, and TKM in a similar fashion saw that, to retrieve anything at all of their investment, they would have to reopen talks with Mike Donoghue.

Fifteen

How Michael Donoghue Did a Deal with TKM Despite a Late Scare

There is a general perception that management buy-outs represent a licence (for those managers fortunate enough to have the chance) to make a fortune. The reality is rather different. As with the lottery, those you hear about are the winners. The losers, who have probably taken second mortgages on their houses, put their wives on the street, and sold their children into slavery in an attempt to save a failing business and their jobs, are simply not newsworthy. And yet, having reminded ourselves that there are losers, we have to concede that there are also winners, and some of them win spectacularly. They succeed where a larger, stronger organisation has failed because they know the business better, because they are prepared to work all hours to ensure its success and, above all, because they are using their own cash. As we all know, no use of resources is as wasteful as that done with other people's money for the supposed benefit of third parties. Conversely, no money is more carefully used than your own in your own business.

Three of the Taunton companies we have talked about so far, Avimo (briefly), Taunton Cider and Langdons, were all involved in management buy-outs: not because beneficent owners wished to reward managers who had made them wealthy (although that was indeed how the generous Frenchman Henri Feuillée acted when he sold Avimo) but because previous attempts to sell the businesses on satisfactory terms to third parties had failed. We need not delve too deeply into the Avimo case, which happened as long ago as 1966, before a management buy-out would have been recognised as a concept or had turned into the acronym MBO so widely used today. Avimo is only of interest in this story because it involved two of the parties who, 20 years later, were to have a role in the sale of Langdons by TKM.

After failing to find a buyer for Avimo on behalf of M. Feuillée (and I don't recall trying very hard), I was introduced to two young partners of a small London merchant bank. They constructed a deal whereby I bought the business myself and immediately floated it with a full stock market quotation through the Cardiff Stock Exchange (now long gone), immediately obtaining a quotation in London also. One of those bankers was Richard Cox-Johnson. In those innocent times, there were no reduced share prices for insiders or hidden fees for the promoters. I wrote the contract to sell and buy Avimo between myself and M. Feuillée in French on a single sheet of paper, unblessed by lawyers or accountants, and we both signed it. Ah, those were the days! Six years later Avimo was itself taken over in a friendly deal with Peter (Lord) Levene. As all the investors, including a majority of the employees, had multiplied their capital by a factor of five, and the future of the firm in Taunton was guaranteed, there were no complaints. After the take-over, Avimo went on to achieve still greater success, and remains the town's largest employer, if you don't count the bureaucrats—and it would take you an unconscionable time to count them all these days.

You may have already picked up the fact that Michael Donoghue had asked me to help him in his negotiations with TKM. It is always sensible for a manager to use an outsider under these circumstances. The prospective buyer needs someone who is objective, to prevent him making a rash offer or being bullied by a vendor who is also his boss. If the offer is successful, he will need help in putting the deal to bed, including raising finance. If it fails, and he has to continue to live with the owner, he needs someone to blame as a scapegoat.

We met because one of Michael's children, one of Gordon Copley's children and one of mine were in the same class at the same school. Gordon was Michael's next-door neighbour and worked for a firm of head-hunters with an office in Bristol, which was managed by John Henderson, whom I knew from working together on a number of occasions since our first contact in the darkest days of Rolls Royce and its receivership. I had also spent two years offering advice to the head office of the head-hunting firm itself after it ran into difficulty in its West End operation. None of the problems, I hasten to add, was attributable to the very competent John Henderson, Gordon Copley or the Bristol office.

As a company called West Monkton Advisory Services Ltd (WMAS) forms part of the Langdons saga, a mention of its origins and methods is unavoidable. In 1975, I had stopped working for any one employer and usually had half a dozen or so permanent jobs, divided between quoted companies and public bodies, coupled with incidental work advising firms which had run into problems. For most people, doing a management buy-out or trying to save a company which is in trouble is a one-off experience which they do not want to repeat. If, however, you have done it, or tried to do it, many times, you hope to have learned by your mistakes. With luck you may also have built up goodwill among bankers and other investors who are more likely to accept your recommendations than those of a novice when it comes to putting up some cash. You know what questions they are likely to ask, and prepare your answers in a business plan they will find it simple to understand and verify.

The work was fascinating but was made almost impossible for an individual to carry on because of the tax regime then in force. Income tax on personal earnings was at 84 per cent, making it difficult to save for investment. Travel and hotel expenses were also taxed as income, if the job was distant from your home, because the Revenue classified them as 'travel to work'. On government duty, the Treasury grossed the expenses up so that the net amount received by the person who had incurred the expense was fully recovered, at standard tax rates. For those who paid tax above those rates, however, the cost, for example, of attending monthly Board meetings at the other end of the country exceeded the net amount of the salary. If you invested personally in a recovery situation, the interest on any borrowed money was not allowable as a deduction for tax purposes but the dividends on the investment were taxed at 98 per cent.

(My trade union colleague on the English Industrial Estates Corporation, the likeable Joe O'Hagan, who had been President of the TUC, got round the punitive taxing of his expenses by combining trips on Corporation business with those he made as a member of the nationalised Iron and Steel body. By charging twice for each journey, he managed to stay slightly ahead of the game.)

Denis (Lord) Healey boasted that he would squeeze the rich until the pips squeaked. Had he known more about citrus fruit, he would have found out that, if you squeeze pips, they fly off somewhere else, and it has been a source of some regret that hundreds of the jobs created or saved in part at least by the activities of WMAS have been and are abroad, and that hundreds of millions of dollars earned by those foreign companies have not benefited the United Kingdom except the comparatively tiny amounts paid as fees and dividends to WMAS. However, when you choose to fire grapeshot down a crowded street, you don't merely injure the one or two villains in the crowd.

As the requests for help or advice kept arriving, my friend (Sir) Harry Moore, the wisest of men, suggested it would be more practicable for me to operate through a company than to try to carry on as an individual. That is why WMAS was formed in 1978 with a capital of £100 subscribed by me and my children.

WMAS had several advantages. In the immediate family we had two solicitors and two Chartered Accountants, one of each in practice. This meant we could check things out, prepare documents, agree business plans and so on without the delay, expense and boilerplate which are inevitable if you use outsiders. We were also able to detect and deflate pomposity, unnecessary complication, and sometimes plain sharp practice when it was threatened or displayed by the solicitors and accountants retained by the other side. As we never had any offices, telephone number, advertising, borrowing or employees, we didn't have to charge for advice unless there was a continuing commitment on our part. We could also afford to work only for people we liked and trusted.

Because its income was no longer taxed at the rate applicable to an individual, WMAS was before long able to give confidence to outside investors by putting its own money into propositions it recommended, although it always did so on the terms available to outsiders and not through any 'sweetheart deals'. If I was asked to stay with the investment at the request of the management, a bank, or the outside investors, WMAS stipulated that there could be no commitment on either side: I could, and can, leave or be fired at any time without any notice or compensation.

The disadvantages of WMAS were that frequently there was too much to do involving too much travel, and that people expect miracles. I once met Paul Sheane, the head of Shannon Development, as we were leaving a plane in Dublin: one of the nicest things about the last 25 years has been never to have been without an assignment in Ireland. Instead of greeting me, Paul asked 'What is the secret?' Standing in line to disembark in the aisle of a small aeroplane was not the time or place to say other than, 'There is none'. WMAS had, however, learned that, if a business is losing money, there are only four things you can do, which are:

* Increase volume without increasing fixed costs
* Reduce fixed costs without losing volume
* Increase prices without losing sales
* Shut down

As soon as you realise there are only five variants to logic problems, they are easier to solve. So too with problem companies, where the variables are one less. In practice, you may have to do a bit of each, but the objective analysis is simple once you realise you are only looking for these four things. As we noted earlier, a diagnosis is easy, a cure less so, and applying the medicine hardest of all. The treatment, however appropriate, will not work if the manager in charge of the operation is incompetent.

After going through the Langdon figures together, Michael Donoghue and I spoke to Richard Cox-Johnson who had moved on to be Chairman of another merchant bank and with whom WMAS had since done various deals. He thought that, at the price we proposed to offer, the finance could be arranged. We agreed also to involve other investment advisers, Simon Ashton and Charles Breese, who acted for a source of finance called the Growth Fund. The Growth Fund was owned by two insurance companies, the Friends Provident and UK Provident, and had the advantage for the firms in which it invested that it did not start looking for an exit, and a quick profit, the moment it bought some shares. In my experience, only 3is among the firms which describe themselves as venture capitalists shows similar judgment, maturity and restraint, which may be why it is so successful.

I have had to check my diaries to verify the dates which follow. Among the various things which came up and which seemed significant at the time, I have to confess that, in the week in which Michael first asked me to join him in the acquisition of Langdons, I did not give my nascent involvement much prominence. What is that adage about acorns and oak trees? I was far more excited at being asked by the Chief Executive of the Wessex Water Authority to write a paper to submit to the Secretary of State on the question of privatisation.

If a parent company sells a subsidiary, it usually remains liable for its debts for a period of 12 months, which stops people bilking their creditors by passing ownership to a man of straw. It is normal therefore for the vendor to take a look at the projections and financing of the prospective owners. As a result, having submitted our offer, I duly went on 6 April 1983 to see a director of TKM to go through our plans and figures with him. He was unhappy that we had elected not to take over an onerous lease at Arnos Castle and indicated that the sum we were offering was £125,000 less than he would be able to recommend. A week later our offer was formally rejected and we learned that TKM had decided not to sell, proposing instead to implement the business plan we had prepared, of which I had left a copy. I had by now also met TKM's Managing Director and he offered WMAS a contract to visit all the other transport businesses and make suggestions about them. As my knowledge of the industry was scanty and the business plan had in effect been based on Mike Donoghue's input, and that of his Finance Director, Bill Wallace, this did not seem a good idea.

The first ten months of 1984 continued to show poor results at Langdons. On 20 November TKM made a fresh approach to Michael Donoghue for an offer. Again the asking price was too high, although Richard Cox-Johnson said he could still put a deal together despite the losses if the price were right. It was left to me to have that unsatisfactory conversation with the TKM 'Disposals Manager' on 14 January 1985 in the presence of Mike Donoghue and Bill Wallace. Bill was depressed by what had happened and, thinking that we would never do a deal with TKM, he decided to leave. His replacement, Paul Rowe, had been with Langdons since 1975 and, although not an qualified accountant, was familiar with every aspect of the administration and possessed with a vast store of common sense. To fill the perceived gap caused by the departure of Bill Wallace and reassure our potential investors, my eldest son Rob Holder, an accountant member of WMAS, was made available as a part-time (unpaid) Financial Director, although Paul Rowe and David Every-Clayton did most of the work.

For eight months after the departure of Bill Wallace, TKM urgently and unsuccessfully sought an outside buyer for Langdons. They knew that closure would be extremely costly and on 27 September 1985, having failed to interest anyone else, they again invited Michael Donoghue to make a bid. We decided to let TKM sweat for a few weeks, and then went back on 20 November with a figure £500,000 less than what they had previously suggested, although we did agree to take on the Bristol leases. On 23 December the deal was agreed in principle and everything stopped for Christmas and the New Year. On 10 January, 1986 we received from TKM some outline Heads of Agreement in gobbledegook, which we redrafted. These were signed on 29 January, and we were at last faced with the reality of asking our supporters to honour their pledges and get the cash in our bank.

We now had to obtain independent verification of the projections we had made for turning a loss-making business into profit, and so persuading outsiders to risk their money in the business. The loss for 1985 was projected to be in excess of £300,000 and, although this included an element of 'kitchen-sinking', there was no way of pretending that Langdons was an ongoing profitable concern. ('Kitchen-sinking' is the accounting convention whereby you include in the Profit and Loss Account every contingency and provision you can think of, to make the figures look as bad as possible.) Preparing accounts showing a sorry situation did not present Paul Rowe with a substantial difficulty because, with Langdons in 1985, there were plenty of losses and very few profits.

Using the tested formula of cutting costs, increasing profitable turnover, raising prices, and closing loss-makers, Michael Donoghue arrived at figures projecting a turnover in 1986 reduced by almost £2 million but a profit improvement (or mainly a loss reduction) of £450,000. The next stage was to convince others that all this was not a pipe dream, which is why you then call in reporting accountants to check your figures and assumptions, and to make an independent report. Having worked closely with Tom Allen, a shrewd senior partner in Peats, for many years, I asked him to do the job. Unfortunately he was busy and had to delegate it to one of his team.

We received the draft Report some 66 pages long on 5 March. It was beautifully typed and nicely laid out, but entirely useless for our purposes. Many of the phrases will be familiar to professional men and women who are expert in covering their backs against possible future claims:

'Langdons is, to a certain extent at least, a new and as yet untested business.'

'The Company … does not have the benefit of any long-term contracts.'

'None of the information (on which the report was based) has been verified by us.'

'We have not sought to confirm the reasonableness or commercial validity of the assumptions on which the forecasts are based and accordingly express no opinion on whether the forecasts are achievable.'

I spoke to Tom Allen expressing my dismay at the draft. As the person who drafted it has now achieved an eminent position in his profession, not excluding a tap on his shoulder from the Queen, I will not repeat here what Tom's response was. Happily there was still enough time to enable Charles Breese to do a thorough job, and his report, some 20 pages long, was in our hands on 24 March, not hedged about with reservations and boilerplate, but giving a fair assessment of what we had in mind, and the financial consequences.

In a going concern, the debtors are almost always larger than the creditors and in the case of Langdons the difference was about £150,000. When you buy a business with its inventory, you in effect have a holiday of six weeks before you have to start paying any debts, and TKM agreed to lend Langdons this amount to be repaid with interest over a three-year period. There was also the sum of £150,000 outstanding in respect of the conversion of the temperature-controlled store at Arnos C in Bristol, and we agreed to repay this, without interest, over a period of ten years. Under TKM, Langdons had an overdraft with Midland Bank which was estimated at £540,000, and the buyers agreed to repay this also. The only cash which had to pass to TKM on completion would be £8,000. In total, the price represented a discount of £271,000 against the net assets of the company.

Although completion was delayed until March 1986, the operative date was 31 December 1985, and this is where some of the 'kitchen-sinking' came in. The estimated losses for the first three months of 1986 were thrown back into the previous year, along with the closure and redundancy costs associated with shutting the depots in Spalding, Fareham, London and Manchester, and a few other items like a dilapidation claim on a warehouse at the old SRD in Norton Fitzwarren.

To finance the deal, and in effect buy assets of just under £1 million, the buy-out team had to find £725,000. Of this TKM were leaving behind £150,000 on loan, £200,000 was to be lent by a bank, £250,000 was to be introduced by outside investors (mainly the Growth Fund with a contribution also from WMAS) and the balance of £125,000 by the subscription for ordinary shares of £1 each by Michael Donoghue, Rob Swindells and Paul Rowe. The bank loan was arranged through an old friend, Peter Dobbs, the Regional Director and General Manager for the south west of Lloyds Bank based in Salisbury, and a very shrewd banker. Peter was a trifle surprised when, on 26 March, I had to tell him that the Peat's report was unsatisfactory and we had gone elsewhere. However neither then, nor later, did he waver in his support for the buy-out team or for Langdons under its new owners. For our part we have been happy to have been able to repay his confidence, and his bank.

All was ready for completion on 27 March 1986, the day before Good Friday—apart from final confirmation of the loan from the Growth Fund. With no positive news, we were able to put off settlement until after Easter, despite growls and grumbles from the grand but dismissive lawyer acting for the vendor. Richard Cox-Johnson in his usual positive manner said he would see us through 'one way or another'. The following Tuesday, on 1 April, Charles Breese told us that the Growth Fund had decided not to proceed, leaving us the April fools with a hole of £250,000 in our financing. Of this sum, £63,000 was to have been loan capital. We decided to make up the deficit by issuing more ordinary shares at £1.50 each, as against the £1 paid by the three executive directors. Michael Donoghue's father came forward with a substantial amount of cash. Richard Cox-Johnson, Charles Breese and one of their associates, Stephen Keynes, all made major contributions. The deficit was narrowed down within 24 hours to £45,000, and WMAS agreed to take 30,000 additional shares to make up the total. We were thus able to complete the purchase on 2 April 1986, as though there had never been a crisis.

On 7 April UK Provident, one of the proprietors of the Growth Fund, was reported as being in difficulty with the authorities over its liquidity ratio. It would have been helpful, and less stressful, if they had warned us they might be having problems a little sooner.

Sixteen

HOW LANGDONS WENT BACK INTO PROFIT
AND THE LICENSED TRADE

So it was that the team at Langdons under Michael Donoghue completed the management buy-out, despite the shock of having to fill a hole £250,000 deep in 24 hours. That was not the end of the story, or even an occasion for celebration, but another hazardous beginning. The need to return the company to profitability was the more urgent because the people who had come to the rescue at short notice—Richard Cox-Johnson, Charles Breese, Stephen Keynes and Michael Donoghue's family—could not be expected to leave their money in the business in the longer term, as had been the implicit agreement with the Growth Fund. That meant that any plans involving capital expenditure would have to be postponed until these generous people had been generously repaid.

The management had been changed in a number of ways since the old guard had left, giving people more clearly defined areas of responsibility. After the loss of Bill Wallace, Paul Rowe took charge of finance (aided by David Every-Clayton) along with control of the owner-driver accounts, on which regular losses had been incurred in the past and would continue so long as the company could not afford to buy its own tractors. Rob Swindells had become Sales Director in addition to remaining in charge of operations. The control of the traffic office was split, with the sturdy, dependable and totally committed figure of Christopher Murt, who had joined the company at Avonmouth, taking over all the ambient side of the business. Christopher, who is now Langdons' Director of Operations, was to become a key figure in the firm's development. Rupert Ryall, lately returned from Fareham when the depot there was closed, worked with Christopher in the Traffic Office, concentrating on temperature-controlled transport.

It may be appropriate to interpose here, for those not familiar with the transport business, what being a traffic operator involves. He (or in the case of Pip Woodman and the other ladies doing the job, she) has to find full outward loads for all the vehicles under his charge, and agree rates. He must see that the drivers take their statutory rests. He must ensure that the loads match the capacity of the vehicle in terms of bulk and weight. He must calculate transit times and ensure that drops (deliveries to customers) are made within the time window given by the customer. He must plan ahead so that, when a vehicle has made a delivery, another suitable load is available nearby. He must avoid the temptation of dispatching vehicles with less than full loads, which erodes profit. If there are delays on the roads or at customers' premises, he must juggle his timetables and warn of possible delays. If a load has not been delivered in the allotted slot, he must tell the customer immediately and, until a new delivery time can be agreed, make sure that the goods are properly stored. He must ensure that all tachographs are properly used in the vehicles, and check them for discrepancies, comparing them with drivers' time-sheets and the journeys they have undertaken. He must see that all POD (proof of delivery) documents are returned in respect of every load. He must check drivers' hours, fuel consumption, and other expenses. He must be sure to have tractors and trailers available to the home garage for mandatory regular inspections. He must keep in mind on a rolling basis information on all these elements for up to forty vehicles at any time, all over the United Kingdom and perhaps in Europe, hour after hour, day after day, knowing where they are, how many hours the drivers have left before a break, what they are carrying, when they will tip, where their next load is. And then there are the occasional breakdowns. Compared with a transport-traffic operator, an air-traffic controller may be considered to lead the life of Riley.

Michael Donoghue's analysis in planning the future of Langdons took account of three of the four solutions which we noted earlier as being available to a business which is losing money. The fourth, perhaps the easiest, putting up prices without losing sales, was not practicable because none of Langdons' customers, even Varma with its paper and ICI with its fertiliser, had any binding commitment to continue trading with the company and their business remained always under competitive threat. There was also the problem that the biggest customer in 1985, Smedleys, had disappeared as soon as the Spalding depot was closed on 31 March 1986.

Another of the four options, closing down the business (or bits of it), was immediately implemented in London and Manchester as well as in Spalding. The idea behind the depots in London and Manchester had been to secure return traffic to the west of England. These sites were expensive to operate and difficult to manage from afar. Both had been consistently losing money and, with Rob Swindells partly dedicated to sales and marketing, customer liaison could be better done by telephone from Walford Cross, or through personal visits. Fareham, which had been established to hold the Maidment business, presented a different problem. Langdons wanted to stay in chilled distribution but, without a modern and reliable fleet and with no chilled warehousing other than in Bristol, Fareham had become a liability.

Another source of trimming costs was by reducing the excessive amount of 'running light', the miles covered by the vehicles without a payload. We saw that in 1984 the chipboard manufacturer, Aaronsons in South Molton, had been the biggest customer. Aaronsons had dropped to number six in 1985 but still enjoyed in its yard the complementary presence of a shunter and driver provided by Langdons. There was virtually no outward traffic from Taunton into the wilds of Exmoor, which made the rates Langdons was able to charge uneconomic because of keen competition for the chipboard traffic with the local hauliers, who could get return loads to the Barnstaple area. Once Michael Donoghue decided to cut costs on the Aaronson account by removing the shunter, it was only a matter of months before the rest of the business disappeared too.

The staple business of transport operators, particularly those selling 'wheels' only in the most competitive sector of the market, is traffic which they load close to their home base, so that at the very least they are carrying a full payload on their outward journeys. For Langdons, the absence of this base load remained a serious problem. Much of what the firm classified as 'outward' involved excessive empty running, of which the most significant was the carriage of Lucozade and Ribena from the Beecham's plant at Coleford in the Forest of Dean, half an hour beyond the Severn Bridge. It was not that there was no regular outward traffic available from the west Somerset area: the trouble was that Langdons had failed to capture much of it. And of course the greatest prize would be Taunton Cider, seven miles away in Norton Fitzwarren.

Langdons also needed to reduce its rent bills. In Bristol it had reluctantly accepted the liability of the warehouses at Arnos Castle as part of its deal with TKM. The temperature-controlled Arnos C continued to produce a reasonable return, especially after all the capacity was taken by a single customer, Tom Granby, as its south-western distribution depot. Arnos B, however, was too elaborate and therefore too expensive to use for the storage of dry goods, especially when there was limited revenue from handling, cross-docking (taking stuff in and out), and haulage to and from the store. So long as the Dock Labour Scheme compelled suppliers and users of newsprint and other paper to carry buffer stocks as an insurance against random strikes, part of Arnos B would be needed to store the two- and three-ton reels which Varma imported from Finland. There was a brief flurry of profitable activity caused by the last of the dock union actions (or inactions) before the Thatcher reforms came into effect, after which Arnos B remained a constant drag and loss-maker until Langdons managed to get shot of it under circumstances which we will come to later.

Langdons also had two warehouses under lease at the SRD in Norton Fitzwarren, one tenancy expiring in March 1986 and the other continuing until 1991. There was no way of avoiding crippling dilapidations on the first of these, made the more galling by the knowledge that the sum claimed would never be reinvested in repairs to the building, but alleviated in part (as we saw) by throwing much of the cost back on to TKM. To avoid the same problem with the second store of some 35,000 square feet, Michael Donoghue renegotiated the lease by eliminating the dilapidation clause in return for reducing the period of entitlement to occupy. The owners of the estate agreed to this because they expected to redevelop it for housing long before 1991. They should have known better where planning consents are concerned. They are still living in hope, so I believe.

The other obvious area for reducing costs was in the operation of tractors and trailers. As we have noted, new kit is more profitable than old, and buying equipment is preferable to renting it. With the permitted loading of refrigerated articulated trailers increasing, Langdons decided to carry on renting until it was clear what the maximum was likely to be, and so avoid owning equipment which would become obsolescent as the Regulations changed. The five trailers Michael bought in 1981 carried 18 pallets each, which was then the legal limit. He resisted buying any more temperature-controlled trailers until the standard had reached 26 pallets. Obsolescence apart, it would not have been sensible to have entered the market in the interim because that would have landed the traffic controllers with a mixed fleet. As we just observed, their life is complex enough without having to mix and match trailers to loads on an hourly basis according to their carrying capacity.

Fortunately at the time of the acquisition, Langdons owned 46 flat-bedded or curtain-sided trailers apart from the 10 it leased. It was clearly sensible to cut out the hiring as soon as possible, but that meant either finding cash for buying, or credit for obtaining hire-purchase, and neither of these commodities was readily available to the firm in April 1986, although Lloyds Bank never demurred at financing the firm before Peter Dobbs retired.

The position with tractors for the articulated rigs was dire. At the buy-out Langdons owned two only, apart from the three old dogs which were untaxed and used for shunting in the yard and at Aaronson's. Despite the dangers inherent in guaranteeing the accounts of owner-drivers and the lack of control which the company inevitably has over their operations, there was no alternative, if the fleet were to be renewed and made more reliable, to putting resources into the owner-driver scheme rather than buying company vehicles. The strategy was discussed with Peter Dobbs and eventually credit of £1.4 million was granted by the bank specifically for the purchase of vehicles by owner-drivers. It was to be some years before the improved finances of the firm allowed the policy to be modified so that the balance moved in favour of company-owned vehicles. Although the improvement in the quality of the tractors led to greater reliability, reduced repair costs and a better image for the customers, it also led to constant losses through having to fund owner-drivers who lost money and were unable to clear their debts when they sold up and left to do something else.

The fourth area for the managers to examine was that of increasing sales without increasing fixed costs. Obviously, if the warehouses were full and the vehicles all on the road, there was unlikely to be much scope for more profit generation in those areas in the short term. However the company occupied a freehold site at Walford Cross adjacent to the M5 motorway midway between junctions 24 and 25, and at the point where the A38 and A361 trunk roads meet. The average daily number of heavy goods vehicles using the M5 was 3,450, with another 940 on the A38, and commercial traffic was growing at around 3 per cent per year. The only local lorry park was four miles away, at the cattle market beside the railway station in Taunton, where there were no facilities other than a nearby hostelry which was said to offer a 'grab a granny night' every Thursday. With so little outward traffic from Taunton, most of the Langdons' vehicles spent the nights during the week away from base, leaving empty spaces for visiting drivers, who would pay for parking and for any other services of which they might avail themselves.

The planning authorities were happy at the prospect of keeping heavy vehicles out of Taunton and welcomed the idea of setting up a Truck Stop at Walford Cross. Fortunately a private house came on the market adjacent to the company's offices, its price blighted by its industrial neighbour. With the bank's help, Langdons bought the house and its former offices were converted into a restaurant, washing facilities, a shop, a hairdresser's, a recreation area, and a bar which was given a full licence to sell alcohol. With the prospect of much increased fuel sales, an auction took place between two oil companies for the right to supply diesel on an exclusive basis for a period of five years. The winner paid enough to finance the development of the Truck Stop, and a brewer was similarly induced to pick up the tab for fitting out the bar. (In case you are surprised at a Truck Stop getting a liquor licence, I am happy to report that, during its decade of operation, there was no single instance of any driver or other customer committing an offence connected with alcohol.)

To stay with the Truck Stop, even at the risk of getting ahead of ourselves, during the course of the exclusive supply agreement the oil company with whom Langdons had done the deal ran into difficulties stemming from the insolvency of its American parent. Its plans to develop a network of Truck Stops in the United Kingdom were abandoned and it agreed to release Langdons from its tie, subject to repayment of part of the advance. Langdons then entered into a similar deal with BP, who were investing in this market sector, and thereby financed the building of 14 bedrooms, for which planning permission was only secured by a majority of one. Perhaps the councillors found it difficult to accept the idea of a truck driver sleeping between sheets in a comfortable bed with his own colour television and washing facilities. A further development, the establishment of a snooker room with two full-sized tables, proved less successful.

As the reputation of the Truck Stop grew, and it was certainly unlike any other, so the pressure for parking space became a problem, coinciding as it did with the belated expansion of Langdons' transport business. Two adjoining fields were available for purchase, which would have provided another seven acres of ground. Against the sage advice of Peter Dobbs, who offered to fund the purchase of both plots, the Board agreed to buy only one and when later a price had been agreed for the other, they were gazumped by a neighbouring car-breaker, leaving no more than 10 acres in all on the site: which was enough until it became necessary to keep adding to the warehouses, and the number of Langdons' vehicles moved above a hundred.

Apart from offering unrivalled facilities to visiting drivers, the Truck Stop acted as a canteen and ablutions for Langdon employees, and as a club where everyone in the firm could meet over a pint (or more) of beer and chew the fat. One year it was voted 'Truck Stop of the Year' by a poll in a trade paper. I don't know if there were any other candidates, and I would be ashamed to tell you how few votes were actually cast for the winner. But it sounded good. The Truck Stop also made money from the outset, mainly from the much increased sale of fuel. The Descriptive Memorandum prepared by Charles Breese at the time of the buy-out had been optimistic in its estimate of the number of visiting lorries which would be accommodated on the site. There would never have been room for 150 overnight, as was suggested. The very peak figure was around 100 for four nights a week but, because many of the drivers used the vehicle wash, had minor repairs done, filled with fuel and then with food, tea and beer, the average year-round overnight figure of 70 was profitable, without taking into account the 300 or so drivers who pulled in during the day for a meal or fuel, or usually both.

We will come eventually to the sad day when the pressure of new and more profitable business caused the Truck Stop to be knocked down and the unusual but much appreciated facility no longer existed. It had worked because it was in the right place, and because it offered drivers the quality of food and service, and the cleanliness, which you would look for in a medium-class hotel. The water was always hot in the free showers and the toilets were cleaned several times a day. There was junk food, including a monster, or monstrous, fried all-day breakfast, but what sold best were the dishes prepared by the chef on site - cottage pie especially in winter, and salads in summer.

Not unexpectedly, the instant success of the Truck Stop was easier to achieve than developing a sick transport business with expensive outside rented warehouses into the kind of coordinated logistics business which Michael Donoghue, Paul Rowe, Rob Swindells and Christopher Murt could only dream about. There were many years of neglect to make good and so long as the firm was unable to offer the kind of integrated service available from its competitors, it would have to stick with 'wheels' only, the simple, but badly paid, end of the business. A transport firm makes real money by taking over all the distribution functions from the customer, ideally accepting the product from the production line, storing it, picking it, trunking it and then making the final deliveries. To do that you need good equipment, racked stores, nationwide connections, a sophisticated IT system and, above all, credibility. In 1986 Langdons had none of those things.

Richard Cox-Johnson was delighted with the success of the Truck Stop and felt that there would be a brighter future for Langdons if it went down that road of development rather than just staying in transport. He may well have been right but the secret to the success at Walford Cross was that the site was already owned, and the Truck Stop revenue was additional to that from the transport operation already carried out there, which was already picking up the fixed overheads. To buy other sites or other Truck Stops would cost money the firm did not have, although it did look at a couple before deciding to concentrate on transport. There was also a question of how to manage a remote site, with all the complications that accompany the running of a cash business. Paul Rowe, and then Clare Langley (now Langdons' Quality Control Manager), kept a tight grip on the restaurant, bar and retail business which was being run on the firm's doorstep but even then there were occasions when the Z registers on the tills (which provide a check not seen by staff) and the cash were not in complete harmony. Langdons was not that endowed with able managers as to be able to send either of them away to run another Truck Stop, especially when the transport side started to grow again.

As with all businesses, doors opened and others shut. The Aaronson's account was lost. With the arrival of milk quotas and the ban on nitrates, the ICI business diminished year by year until that too went and the dedicated warehouse at Norton Fitzwarren was closed. Tom Hewett's old meat-haulage side received a boost when Langdons picked up a major account based in Chard, but the days of carrying hanging carcasses on hooks were fast being replaced by pre-packed joints for supermarkets, which can be carried by anyone who has a standard vehicle. Gradually the Langdons' equipment improved, and company drivers increasingly took their place alongside a diminishing number of owner-drivers. The Taunton Cider account, first obtained in 1986, provided just the kind of outward ambient traffic the firm needed, and the business received a further fillip when Relyon in Wellington, some 15 miles away, developed a foam for household furniture which was bulky in content but very light and did not asphyxiate every member of the household if the sofa caught fire. To complement this increased outward traffic, Rob Swindells, with the able traffic operators Christopher Murt and Rupert Ryall, found customers for regular return traffic to the extent that trailers were often as well laden coming home as they were going out. By 1990, Rob was able to concentrate wholly on sales, with Christopher taking charge of both transport and warehousing.

Yet problems remained. The rent at Arnos B rose inexorably. All attempts to win a major customer requiring a logistics service failed because Langdons had no suitable racked storage. The only success in that direction was with a small company in which WMAS held an interest, supplying the UK market with a product made by a Norwegian company which WMAS happened also to have advised some years previously. Langdons found itself back again with chickens and eggs. How do you entice a customer to entrust his business to you if you have no suitable facility, and how can you afford the facility without any customers?

In 1988 the investors who had so nobly helped Michael Donoghue out in April 1986 expressed their wish to recover their investment and leave the company. Through an ingenious scheme about which the auditors and lawyers were uncertain but which had the full backing of Peter Dobbs, the three executive directors were able to buy back all the shares which had been issued at the last moment, giving their rescuers a handsome profit. The need to recoup this unplanned payment inevitably slowed the growth and re-equipment of the company, but at least the firm was back in the hands of the four original parties to the buy-out, with Michael Donoghue having the biggest share.

Seventeen

HOW TAUNTON CIDER WON PROSPERITY
AND LOST INDEPENDENCE

The management buy-out of Taunton Cider was more complicated than the Avimo case, which we noted briefly, and infinitely more so than what happened with Langdons. The company was of course much bigger than Avimo or Langdons had been but times too had changed. Gone were the days of innocence or naivety when the employees and their advisers took their stakes during an MBO on the same terms as outsiders. Handled with care, a management buy-out in the early 1990s was a chance, their only chance perhaps, for managers to make their fortunes overnight. It was also an opportunity for their advisers in the City of London to keep themselves in the manner to which they had become accustomed; added to which there might also be the opportunity to repay a few favours and indulge in that mutual back-scratching without which no self-respecting financial centre could prosper.

The Taunton Cider buy-out was managed internally by three of Taunton's directors, Peter Adams, Brian Longstaff and Andrew Nash, with the knowledge of Miles Roberts, the Chairman, but without his direct involvement. We have met Messrs Adams and Longstaff earlier, and can only add that they were well regarded and respected within the firm and in the trade. The third member of the triumvirate, Andrew Nash, was in his early '30s and had come to Norton Fitzwarren in 1987 after acquiring his skills with Cadbury Schweppes and honing them with Sterling Health Limited, who were in the 'consumer health care business', as it was described.

We have noted that the shareholders had been trying to sell Taunton Cider to third parties, among whom Cinven, Guinness and Matthew Clark had showed an active interest. Cinven, which managed very substantial pension funds, might perhaps have bought the company with the ultimate intention of selling it on or floating it at a profit, because investment companies don't usually choose to stay with large holdings in unquoted companies for a number of good reasons. An unquoted company is likely to need more supervision, and to be more trouble-prone, than a quoted one, having less need for disclosure as required by the Yellow Book of the Stock Exchange and therefore liable to give its shareholders less information; there is no daily mechanism for telling precisely what its shares are worth, which complicates matters for those shareholders who have in their turn to report figures regularly to their own investors; and there is no easy exit when they wish to cash in all or part of their investment.

Guinness would seem to have been a good choice as buyer. It knew Taunton Cider well, from having had a member on the board and having helped to establish its expertise in brand development. Although Guinness had no tied houses, it knew how to get product into both the pub market and the retail trade. Cider would have been a good fit with its stout and its *Harp* lager. From the point of view of the employees, it was directly interested in no competing business, and unlikely to become so. With its financial muscle, Guinness might have been expected to encourage expansion at Norton Fitzwarren without threatening the reorganisation, retrenchment and redundancies which could follow amalgamation with a company with other interests in cider.

There was, however, that one factor working against Guinness: some of their former partners in Taunton Cider didn't want to sell to them.

The third contender, Matthew Clark, might have thought it had an inside track in the auction. Its Managing Director, Peter Aikens, had been a member of the Taunton board from May 1987 to May 1989 and was keen to add cider-making to his expanding drinks-distribution, wine and British sherry empire. Brewing is an incestuous industry in which most senior people seem to have played musical chairs among the big groups during their careers. Brian Longstaff knew, and was well known by, Matthew Clark. The chosen successor for Miles Roberts as Chairman at Taunton was Michael Cottrell who, like Peter Aikens, had been with Courage when it was a Taunton shareholder, had sat on the Taunton board from 1984 to 1987, and was in 1991 still a director of Matthew Clark.

When the bids came in, the front runner was Guinness, with £86 million on the table. If the buy-out team found out that figure, and it seems more than probable that they did, all they and their advisers had to do was to stitch together a deal which, in total, gave the shareholders a more attractive package than merely pouching £86 million, factored for their prejudice against Guinness, and one which allowed any existing Taunton Cider shareholder who was an unwilling seller to keep his shares in any reconstructed company. That task proved not too difficult, with the help of the merchant bankers, Samuel Montagu, although the buy-out team had to make numerous journeys to London and endure interminable meetings with the bankers and their mandatory professional 'advisers' before the final pattern emerged and all the boilerplate had been fitted. A further requirement of the package was that it had to be tailored so that after a short pause Taunton Cider plc could apply for a listing on the Stock Exchange, or 'go public'. When that happened the outsiders putting up the money for the buy-out and for working capital would be able to realise their investment with, it was to be hoped, some profit in recognition of the risks which they had so courageously taken in lending their support to the manufacturing sector.

The buy-out deal was done on 22 May 1991 and the sellers, including Bass and Courage, received £236.2237 a share. This was a reasonable return, you may think, on the £2.40 or £2.50 which some of them had paid when they joined the company two decades earlier, particularly as much of the consideration may not have been paid in cash but through the transfer of written-down vats and other machinery. Those of you with calculators will have at once realised that this consideration amounted in full to no more than £47,623,642.82p, or rather less than the Guinness offer, but it was paid for no more than 82 per cent of the business and the shareholders had in addition received a special dividend costing £14.5 million net of Advance Corporation Tax. The overall effect was that a price of around £70 million was agreed and gave shareholders the option of taking cash or staying with a company which would shortly have its own quotation. It was also the option which the management preferred.

You will, I trust, forgive me if we stick for a moment to the bare essentials without becoming bogged down in the web of term-loan facilities, an original mezzanine lender, senior and mezzanine underwriting commitments, revolving senior debt, an intercreditor deed, mezzanine warrants, B shares, non-voting ordinary shares, a senior facility agreement, an original senior lender, series 2 loan stock, a debenture, and all the other paraphernalia of so complex a transaction. Under the deal the buy-out team found itself owning, or empowered to distribute among other employees, 6,500,000 shares of 10p each, which they were able to buy at par, or 10p a share. Those of the trade shareholders who stayed aboard invested a further £450,000 while the outsiders, Samuel Montagu and the people they let in on or invited to participate in the deal, acquired their shares at £1 each, or a premium of 90p a share. The effect was initially to leave Peter Adams and his team with about 20 per cent of the company at a cost of £650,000. There was also a ratchet mechanism built into the deal whereby, subject to performance, the employees' share of the equity would be increased by one fifth, giving them effectively 24 per cent of the business. Peter Adams, Brian Longstaff and Andrew Nash kept half of these for themselves and unselfishly made the other half available to other Taunton employees on the same favourable terms, which meant that eventually, when the agreed performance targets had been hit, the three directors held 12 per cent of the equity and the rest of the employees shared the other 12 per cent.

Following the buy-out, at the suggestion of their city advisers who wanted a Finance Director whom they considered 'institutional friendly', the competent Alan Reeve was replaced by Nicholas Pearch; and, as we have seen, Michael Cottrell took over as Chairman from Miles Roberts, although Miles stayed on as a non-executive member of the board.

The new company also decided to sell two of its peripheral products. One was an unsuccessful venture into unfermented apple juice under the name *Copella*, and the other a business selling bottled water flavoured with apple under the name *Piermont*. The *Copella* business was resold to the people from whom Taunton had bought it for the sum of £1 on 3 April 1992 with an additional provision for repayment of inter-company debt, which realised perhaps another million. The *Piermont* brand was sold to another cider maker, Merrydown, for an initial payment of £86,000, with more to come dependent on future sales. Getting rid of *Copella* was no hardship: it had never looked like threatening *Appletise*, the market leader, as a non-alcoholic drink for sale in pubs. *Piermont* was rather different in that it should have given Taunton the opportunity to get into the lucrative bottled-water market. The water used was potable and palatable, coming from a granite aquifer near Redruth in Cornwall, and had it not been for the apple flavouring, the product might have challenged the many brands of bottled water peddled by firms with less expertise in marketing than Taunton Cider, and nothing to match Taunton's existing sales channels.

At the time of the buy-out, the company was seeking to introduce a number of new brands with names such as *Brody*, *Blackthorn Super*, and *Blush*, to add to its old faithfuls like *Special Vat*. *Brody* was not an inspired name you might suppose if your etymological knowledge includes the American phrase to 'do a brodie'. In 1886 Steve Brodie claimed to have jumped off the Brooklyn Bridge into the river below, and to have survived. Despite his escape, to 'do a brodie' came to mean committing suicide by leaping off a high structure. Like Steve, *Brody* survived but, unlike him, did not appear destined to pass into the language.

Special Vat too turned out to have Freudian connotations. While we all know that a seller can be prosecuted by one arm of government for failing to supply a buyer with the quantity specified in the contract, it may come as no surprise that it can also be hounded for covering itself by making sure that the amount sold is slightly greater than the amount specified. In 1991, when Allied Breweries were selling Showerings to the buy-out team headed by John Wilkinson, the Customs and Excise, ever vigilant on our behalf to detect fraud, and flushed with its successful investigation of Matrix Churchill, noticed that a small amount of extra fluid was put in every keg of cider to ensure that it represented the required measure. This of course meant that a heinous offence was being committed, because excise duty was not being paid on the surplus. Rather than postpone the sale to Mr. Wilkinson and his team by entering into a lengthy court action, Allied paid additional duty in the region of £250,000 for the cider they hadn't sold. As the advertisement for biscuits used to say, one bite invites another. When they approached Taunton Cider, the Customs and Excise were looking for unpaid duty amounting to £4 million. They were unfortunate to come up against a resolute and well-informed management and eventually went away with a flea in their collective ear, although not without making a similar approach to Bulmers. Matrix Churchill also turned out to be a Pyrrhic victory, although the compensation of £2 million to the victim was not paid until 1999: but that is another story.

Although Mr. Aikens had failed to win Taunton Cider for Matthew Clark, he was soon successful in acquiring Showerings, where the buy-out had not gone well. As we have already noted, with Showerings came Gaymers, Coates and Whiteways, three venerable names in the cider business although none of them had managed to develop brands with quite the flair of Bulmers and Taunton, except in the far-off days of *Babycham*. Showerings had in *Old English* a volume cider, its popularity perhaps being enhanced by its availability in the 2,500 or so pubs owned by its former parent, Allied Breweries. It also had a *Diamond White* lookalike called *K*.

Meanwhile Taunton were looking to market a new brand of cider which would have a head when poured and look like lager. The product was named *Red Rock* and was planned to take its place beside *Diamond White* and *Autumn Gold* in the public's affections. The colour was achieved but not the head. Ignoring or forgetting how *Diamond White* had been successfully promoted through giving the stuff away until drinkers developed a taste for it, *Red Rock* was launched on the back of an extended and expensive television advertising campaign. At much the same time Bulmers came out with *Scrumpy Jack*, which they launched on the *Diamond White* pattern, through promotions in pubs rather than on the box. *Scrumpy Jack* became a successful brand while *Red Rock* was less so.

The year between the buy-out and the public issue went well for Taunton Cider, with profits before tax and interest increasing from £10.454 million to £17.08 million. As a result of the borrowing to finance the buy-out—all those mezzanine loans and other indebtedness we passed over briefly and amounting in total to nearly £80 million—the company's interest payable to its lenders had risen from £190,000 in the year which ended on 30 April 1991 to £9.611 million in the following April, by which time liabilities exceeded assets by £41.532 million. Turnover was still rising at the rate of £10 million a year. The number of employees had also increased by nine to 512.

All that was needed to restore liquidity was the planned flotation, after which the £41.5 million net liability would be turned into net assets of £23.1 million and the profit before tax but after interest increased (on a pro forma basis) from £7.4 million to £14.8 million. At the issue price of 140p a share, Samuel Montagu and its chosen investors, including Cinven with 7,362,623 shares bought at £1, would not be feeling any pain. As for the buy-out team, they would all be, on paper at least, millionaires. Many of the employees too would show a sizeable profit on their shares, although some at least may have wondered whether that would be enough to pay the bills if the soon-to-be public company were to be taken over by a competitor and they were to lose their jobs. That was not, however, a danger to which the Prospectus drew attention when it listed 'Reasons for the Offer'.

In the placing which took place in July 1992 the directors sold 1,814,265 shares making a profit of 130 pence on each. (You also, as a taxpayer, profited to the extent of 40 per cent of their gain, so it was good news for you as well, perhaps.) The institutional investors sold 6,832,426 shares, making a profit of a little over £27 million with more to come, it must be hoped, when they decided to sell the rest of their holdings. You may feel that Samuel Montagu deserved a more handsome reward for their arduous and successful work and will be gratified to know that

> the costs and expenses of, and incidental to the Offer (of shares) including the cost of the application for listing, accountancy fees and the Company's and Samuel Montagu's legal costs, the costs of printing and advertising the Offer, the fees and expenses of the Receiving Bankers and Registrars and the fees and commissions payable to Samuel Montagu and James Capel & Co Limited by the Company are estimated to amount to £3.1 million (exclusive of VAT).

This was one of the figures with which not all the Taunton Cider management was happy.

As a public company, Taunton Cider plc prospered. It still enjoyed the close relationship with its former shareholders which had been enshrined in medium-term supply agreements. Trade through other retail outlets, especially supermarkets, was expanding. It suffered a serious blow in August 1993 when the much-liked and able Brian Longstaff decided to retire following a tragic bereavement in his family. Brian had for some time been considering the changing pattern of distribution following the switch to non-returnable containers which had started with those disposable glass bottles for *Diamond White*. Once there was no requirement to haul back empties, it no longer made sense to use your own transport in livery (with the company's name and logo on the curtains) because of the difficulty in achieving efficient utilisation without return loads. There was also the prospect of countering union leverage if the lorry drivers and warehouse staff were employed by a third party: no longer could a strike by a few union members outside the factory walls stop production while everyone in the factory continued to draw full wages. If the drivers went on strike, that was the problem of their employer, not yours, and there are always plenty of other transport firms looking for the work.

Brian Longstaff's successor as the Director responsible for logistics, among other things, was Neil Rixon. It had been Neil's decision to start using Langdons as a haulier in 1986 and by 1994 it had proved itself an efficient, competitive and reliable partner. Its closeness to the factory enabled it to respond to changes in demand from hour to hour with a flexibility unmatched by other hauliers, and its high percentage of return loads for third parties meant that its rates were below the cost of using company-owned vehicles manned by Taunton Cider employees. If there were to be a dispute between Langdons and its drivers, that would not affect production in the cider factory, even though those involved might belong to the same union.

With these factors in mind, in 1995 Neil Rixon entered into discussions with Michael Donoghue of Langdons with a view to Langdons taking over every aspect of the distribution of all the cider, including control of the warehouse at Norton Fitzwarren. The deal involved Langdons buying Taunton's tractors and trailers, and taking on as employees its warehousemen and drivers. Langdons instructed lawyers to ensure that the contractual rights of the Taunton Cider employees joining Langdons were properly preserved. Other contracts relating to vehicle maintenance and so on had to be examined and modified as necessary. The transfer of the Taunton Cider logistics to Langdons was due to take place in the autumn. In anticipation, Langdons acquired the additional equipment which would be needed to fulfil its much increased contractual obligations and trained staff so that the transfer would be seamless so far as the factory and the customers were concerned.

Then things appeared to go on hold. The weeks passed and it was proving difficult for Michael Donoghue to tie this major customer down to a written contract or a start date. Meetings were arranged and then postponed. Finding himself by chance on an aeroplane with Peter Adams, Michael discussed the arrangements and received no indication that there might be anything amiss, although Peter Adams, if he was in possession of inside information, was not in a position to say anything. Two or three weeks later an announcement was made that Matthew Clark had made a bid for Taunton Cider. Nothing was said of an intention, if the bid were successful, to curtail the activity at Norton Fitzwarren, nor did Langdons expect any reneging on the distribution deal which had been agreed in principle but not committed to writing and which, like all good contracts, would prove beneficial to both parties. However Taunton Cider was coming under new ownership. Peter Aikens would soon be the Chief Executive in overall charge, not Peter Adams.

In 1994 Langdons had billed Taunton Cider for £779,496 in respect of haulage. The figure rose in 1995 to £1,255,441. If and when Langdons took over all the transport and distribution as agreed, it would grow even more dramatically. How bright the future then looked for Michael Donoghue and his team!

Matthew Clark offered the Taunton Cider shareholders 383 of its own shares for every 1,000 shares in Taunton Cider. When the take-over was completed on 8 November 1995, Matthew Clark shares were trading at 639p each, giving a value of just over 261p for each share in Taunton Cider. Nobody would be so stupid as to imagine that Matthew Clark would pay in effect some £275,000,000 for a business which they were going to change dramatically or shut down, although, as owner of other cider companies, there would obviously be duplication to be avoided, savings to be made—nothing however which a quick dose of P45 medicine would not cure. Nor would anybody be so unrealistic as to turn down Matthew Clark's offer for the Taunton Cider shares at those levels, least of all those in the City who rightly saw themselves merely as trustees of the interests of pensioners, widows and orphans, with no responsibility for the welfare of the inhabitants or the economy of west Somerset.

For a short while nothing changed except that in December the Taunton warehouse and distribution staff learned that they would lose their jobs because it was planned that all the logistics were to be handled from Bristol. Langdons continued to haul up to 40 loads of cider a day from Norton Fitzwarren over the traditionally busy Christmas and New Year weeks. The work dropped as normal in the opening months of 1996 but Langdons still did most of it, without being able to obtain any assurances about what the firm's role might be after the move. Despite an offer of a job with Matthew Clark, Peter Adams decided to retire, as he could well afford to. The local stockbrokers were inundated with selling orders from delighted Taunton employees, many of whom had never before held shares and rejoiced in their new-found wealth.

Walford Cross from the air in 1998.

The price of Matthew Clark dipped, giving the underwriters some unease no doubt, but later recovered. People continued going to work in Norton Fitzwarren as before. For a while for most employees in the factory nothing much seemed to change. It was however gradually dawning on Langdons that the implementation of the distribution agreement was unlikely to happen in the manner previously agreed, if at all.

Eighteen

How Prayers were Answered and Langdons Escaped from Arnos Castle

You may remember that, in the series of negotiations between Michael Donoghue and his employers, TKM, over the sale of Langdons, one of the sticking points had been the leasehold warehouses in Bristol, at Arnos Castle. One of these, Arnos B, was specially built with a high roof and strong floor suitable for storing in high stacks the two and three ton reels of paper imported by the Finnish company, Varma. The rest of the space in Arnos B was sold to whoever came along for dry storage. Some of the products were mountain bikes made in the Far East, which were regularly stolen. Although the police said they thought they knew who the thieves were, the law seemed incapable of preventing return visits to what must have been likened by the burglars to Aladdin's Cave. No doubt the constabulary had weightier concerns on its collective mind. The other warehouse, Arnos C, was the one which had been converted into a temperature-controlled store.

The original rent of £65,600 a year for the two buildings was onerous enough without taking into account the tax charged by Bristol Corporation for the privilege of occupying premises in its fair but traffic-bound city, for which it was not easy to discern any benefit given in return to the taxpayer. It was especially unfortunate that the local authority was unable to find resources, out of the tens of thousands of pounds it collected in rates from Langdons, to provide services such as policing or security. The persistent and systematic thieving from Arnos B further increased the losses by virtue of the claims from customers whose goods, like the mountain bikes or other items likely to fall off a lorry, had disappeared. The residual amount of diesel in the storage tank also turned out on occasion to be less than what would have been expected if fuel had been drawn only by authorised vehicles.

There were other problems in managing these warehouses at a distance from Walford Cross, as there are running any concern without close supervision. In the storage business, it sometimes falls to the warehouseman to dispose of goods which the customer no longer needs. One such occasion occurred with dates in the chilled warehouse, Arnos C, after the firm which had imported them had been unable to sell them and then neglected to pay for the storage. It transpired that not even the monkeys at Bristol Zoo would take them, and dumping several tons of dates in an approved landfill site proved expensive. Langdons were also asked from time to time to dispose of surplus reels of paper. That rarely cost money and more often it was possible to obtain some kind of a price from a firm dealing in redundant stocks, who seemed to prefer payment in notes to the use of a bank account. How they completed their VAT returns without a proper record is another mystery. When the disposal cost Langdons money, the customer storing the paper paid the cost: when the paper was sold at a profit, that normally by agreement should have been kept by Langdons. It was with some regret that the firm discovered that its manager at Arnos Castle had been taking a relaxed view as to the pocket in which such residual profits should rest.

Another abuse which had crept into the Arnos B operation was institutional overtime on Saturday mornings at premium rates. The two warehousemen in Arnos B might

occasionally have had to work over a weekend in an emergency but slack management
had allowed them regularly to carry over
jobs each Friday, for all the world as if they
were employed in the docks. When this
overtime was stopped, the two employees
refused to unload any more containers of
paper because the rolls might have moved
in transit from Finland, and it was therefore
unsafe to handle them. While two men from
Taunton continued to do the job without
any risk to life or limb, a cliché which is for
once appropriate, the Health and Safety
Executive was asked to give its ruling and
advice. In so tricky a matter, it was of course
unreasonable to have expected a rapid
decision. Six weeks later the Executive suggested that it might be better if the containers
were not subject to lateral movement in
transit. Their ruling did not confirm that a
copy had been sent to King Neptune and so
it was not capable of unilateral implemen-

Old-style temperature-controlled storage at Arnos
Castle, Bristol in the 1980s.

tation by Langdons. The two employees, suspended until this Judgement of Solomon was
handed down, were each awarded about £2,000 by an Employment Tribunal.

Management, workers and thieving apart, the thing about Arnos B was that it was
simply too expensive to use as a store for dry goods. Week after week, in the detailed
log Michael Donoghue kept on his desk recording the profit and loss of individual
warehouses, Arnos B showed red ink on an increasing scale. There seemed to be no
relief in sight. I visited the landlords, the Royal Insurance Company, in London shortly
before the rent came up again for review in 1988 but received no comfort from them.
Soon after this visit the Royal transferred the freehold to a property company, the
names of whose directors suggested Middle Eastern connections. That too showed no
inclination to grant either relief or release, and the losses mounted. Naturally it proved
impossible to find anyone to take an assignment of such onerous leases on any terms,
although Michael Donoghue tried that also.

In April 1990, Rob Swindells was reading a Bristol newspaper at home when his
eye lit on a report that the Bristol Development Corporation (BDC) intended to
redevelop a large swathe of Bristol, of which the Arnos Castle warehouses formed a
part. On 18 April, he met the Commercial and Project Directors of the BDC who
confirmed that the scheme was going ahead, that a new spine road would probably
require the demolition of Langdons' warehouses, and that work was planned to start in
about 18 months' time, the summer of 1991. Although Rob expressed concern to them
at the threat to his business, the tears in his eyes were not of sadness but of joy. His
memorandum reporting the meeting ended: 'Company-issue prayer mats will shortly be
distributed to help us get the right decision!'

Who says prayers are not answered? In November 1990 plans were published
which showed that the line of the proposed road passed through sections of both

Langdons' warehouses. In February 1991 the London solicitors to the BDC, Nabarro Nathanson, gave Langdons notice of a public enquiry in connection with a Compulsory Purchase Order. There followed a series of discussions between Mike Donoghue and the BDC in which they suggested that Langdons should at once look for other premises so that they could retain the contracts for the Varma paper and with Tom Granby in the temperature-controlled warehouse. The Varma contract especially continued to be important because, you may recall, it was one of the few in which Langdons did both the carriage and the warehousing. The temperature-controlled warehouse, Arnos C, presented less of a problem. It was not loss-making and Tom Granby did all its own transport, which meant that the removal of the business would only marginally affect Langdons' profits overall.

Following pressure from the BDC's agents, who understood the onus on a claimant to mitigate damage as far as possible, Langdons agreed to rent from 1 September 1991 the warehouse at Unit 13 in the former army RSD in Norton Fitzwarren, the very shed where Michael Donoghue had started his life with Langdons 11 years earlier, so that it could begin storing the reels of Varma paper there rather than at Arnos B. The summer passed without any written commitment from the BDC or its agents to confirm the advice and instructions which they had tendered verbally. When pressed for confirmation, the BDC asked Langdons to take the matter up with their Land Agents but the Land Agents said they could give nothing in writing because they could get no instructions out of the BDC.

As might be expected, through these long months the responsible Secretary of State, Michael Heseltine, was too burdened with affairs of state to confirm the Compulsory Purchase Order. Eventually, on 29 August 1991 Michael Donoghue, tired of watching the game of ping-pong between the BDC and its agents and what appeared to his provincial eyes no less than ministerial indolence, wrote to the Department of the Environment pointing out that he had a business to run and responsibility for the welfare of 140 people, apart from commitments to his customers. He ended his letter with the plea: 'I trust when this matter crosses your desk you could give it your immediate attention'. A reply came on 14 October, just over eight weeks later, in effect passing the ball (or buck) back to the BDC. It is not uncommon for a word to have different meanings in the public and private sector. Who is to tell how immediate is 'immediate'?

On 1 October I had written as Chairman of Langdons to the Chairman of the BDC at some length outlining our problem. Writing as Chairman of a company to the Chairman of another organisation with which executive officers have hitherto been dealing is a channel of communication you need to keep in reserve for when all other avenues have been exhausted. You are almost certain to upset the Chief Executive whose inaction or incompetence you are implicitly criticising, and that proved no less true with the BDC than on other occasions. As a result of my letter, the Department of the Environment woke from its trance. The Chairman of the BDC arranged a meeting for Michael Donoghue and me with himself and his senior officers on 17 October, at which they were at pains to express some disappointment that we had seen fit to trouble the Department of the Environment over what they described as no more than a 'communication problem'. The Chairman emphasised that he was sure all could be settled by agreement and insisted he did not want either side to bring in lawyers. We were authorised not to pay any more rent on Arnos B and asked to invoice the cost of vacating the store by 31 December 1991, which would be met by the BDC. The lease of Arnos B could then be surrendered with a payment to Langdons for its residual value. The Chairman asked for a week's grace in which to confirm these matters in writing and to sort out other outstanding issues, including what was to be done over Arnos C.

I must at this point report that the Chairman of the BDC was and is a well-respected and honourable man who was doing his best to achieve certain objectives within the constraints imposed on the BDC by a system which, established to ensure that public moneys are not wasted, has become so complex that it now has the opposite effect. He was also let down by some of his staff who might not have remained in place had it been a private business.

When by 15 December we had heard nothing, I wrote again to the Chairman. Then, still without any response, I sent him a letter by Recorded Delivery on 24 December 1991 reminding him that the actions of the BDC had destroyed our haulage and storage business in Bristol. I said that we could not operate under such uncertainty and we were therefore taking action on a series of assumptions which included vacating Arnos B on 31 December 1991, debiting the BDC with the cost of running two stores for Varma in parallel, and receiving £28,000 in respect of the value of the lease of Arnos B. I also again offered to enter into discussions over vacating of Arnos C.

On 14 February 1992 the Secretary of State found a moment's respite from his other duties to confirm the Compulsory Purchase Order. Although the BDC had agreed in October that Langdons should not pay any more rent for Arnos B and the keys of the warehouse had been returned formally to the BDC's agents on 31 December, under strict legality rent remained payable until the lease had been formally amended or surrendered. On 6 March, the BDC through its agents invoiced Langdons for £70,125.00 arrears of rent on Arnos B. Michael Donoghue's reaction can be imagined by those not privileged to witness it, as I was. Having been involved with politicians and government departments on previous occasions, I was more aware that what might be seen as malice was no more than the inefficiency, waste and indifference with which official business is so often conducted—what the Bard called 'the law's delay, The insolence of office'. I wrote again to the Chairman on 16 March reminding him that the seven days' grace he had sought the previous October had expired and explaining that it had not been an option for us simply to do nothing when our premises were subject to Compulsory Purchase Orders. In January, I told him, his financial staff had advised Langdons that its invoice for the costs of removal from Arnos B had been passed and would be paid within 30 days: on 13 March, Langdons were told that it would not be paid until he personally had written to me.

Following this letter, the Chief Executive of the BDC asked to meet Michael Donoghue without my being present. On this occasion he had a solicitor from Nabarro, Nathanson, the BDC's lawyers, at his side. This prompted Michael to write on his return: 'While we welcome the help given by your lawyer at the meeting, I would remind you that your Chairman suggested at our meeting of 17th October, 1991 that neither side should instruct lawyers, and we have done as he requested. We are anxious to assist you in reaching a settlement but not at the expense of your having an advantage in any negotiation between us.' As it transpired, the lawyer's presence may have helped. The BDC instructed different Land Agents, although those they had previously used cannot be blamed for the shortcomings of their client. The compensation had to be agreed by the District Valuer and, although his attention to the task 'was delayed by other commitments' as we must expect with such overworked public servants, in July a figure of £140,508.43 was paid to Langdons by the BDC as compensation for the vacation of Arnos B, with a further £18,831.39 to be held by Nathan, Nabarro in respect of VAT. It was not surprising that the BDC, being unregistered for VAT, should have demurred at paying it, although on reflection it might have concluded that the money was merely going from one government pocket into another, albeit under different precepts. But as we know from the Matrix Churchill case that the Customs and Excise do not talk to the Foreign Office, we would be unwise to assume that they communicate with the Department of the Environment.

Langdons achieved the desired result with the BDC over Arnos B because of Michael Donoghue's tenacity and meticulous attention to detail. For our key meeting with the Chairman and his staff on 17 October 1991, Michael had a full synopsis of all that had taken place between the parties since April 1990: who had met whom, who had spoken on the telephone to whom, what had been said, what letters had been written and which answered. At the request of the BDC, he left a copy for their future reference and it was at that stage that the Chairman of the BDC suggested that neither side need instruct lawyers. When it came to justifying the costs of vacating Arnos B, Michael produced files of evidence which occupied three large cardboard boxes. The advice of his brother-in-law, Nick Hill, an experienced Surveyor and Land Agent practising in Chepstow, was of enormous value.

This account indicates in detail—too much detail you may think—how important business is often conducted in the public sector, how public servants accept or shun responsibility, and what is the urgency or delay with which decisions are made and executed. I set it out at length, not with the intention of showing how smart Langdons were, nor to criticise public officials whose feet so often seem to be wading through a field of glue, but to remind others in business that there is no alternative, when dealing with officialdom, but to keep accurate notes, to be sure of your facts, to put everything down in writing, to keep pressing, to remain courteous, and to refuse to be browbeaten. Nothing moves an official to action so quickly as a Recorded Delivery letter saying what assumptions of agreement will be made unless a reply is received within seven days, even if you are so caddish as to deliver it on Christmas Eve. Well, not nothing—a Writ of Mandamus is even more effective, but you must save that for a real emergency.

The Langdons' files on the Compulsory Purchase of Arnos B and C from which I have been refreshing my memory are over five inches thick. Having dragged you though so much detail already, I will spare a reprise on Arnos C except to report that the compensation there, including interest arising from an inexplicable delay in payment but excluding VAT, amounted to £294,229.74, which was transferred on 11 November 1993. The payment for disturbance was a round sum of £275,000. Michael Donoghue and I had attended another meeting with the Chairman of the BDC and his staff to discuss a final settlement. As usual, Michael had with him boxes of paper to justify the amount he was claiming—five of them on this occasion. Eyeing the boxes with some apprehension, the Chairman suggested that our claim of around £300,000 seemed on the high side whereas £250,000 might be more appropriate. I replied that £275,000 might be acceptable. He agreed the figure without further discussion and the boxes remained unopened. We simply took them back to Walford Cross.

Before 1990 an old, smallish, Langdons' customer called Quantock Jams in Bridgwater had been taken over by Gerber Foods, which is the leading manufacturer of packaged fruit juices, most of which are sold to supermarkets under their own brands. With the movement in the trade towards chilled produce, Gerber introduced new lines in chilled citrus fruits, which Langdons picked up from their Bridgwater warehouse by the factory for onward delivery. There were many service problems because Gerber did not have sufficient chilled warehousing space to hold buffer stocks and customers persisted in ordering what they had just sold rather than what the factory happened to be making at the moment. Langdons' lorries were often held up while production for an order could be completed, or forced to make part deliveries. The waiting time played hell with drivers' hours and rest periods.

The solution for both parties would be for Langdons to convert part of its warehouse at Walford Cross into a chilled store where buffer stocks could be held, and preferably with another chamber to hold sub-zero produce, in effect to replicate what had been taken over by the BDC under Compulsory Purchase. Unfortunately this would cost around £275,000, a sum which Lloyds Bank were reluctant to advance, having just suffered a serious loss with the failure of a private haulier, John Dee Transport Ltd, in January 1991. Peter Dobbs, having retired, was no longer in charge at Lloyds and the powers-that-be in Lombard Street had decided that, far from providing more finance for private hauliers, the Bank's exposure to them should be reduced. It was later to change its mind about Langdons, but customers look for consistency: if a bank decides it doesn't want all your business, you have to make other arrangements, even if that includes renting equipment for a while. Having made other arrangements, it is wise to keep them in place in case the wind in the City of London again blows from a different direction.

It was lucky for Langdons that the cost of the conversion of the warehouse at Walford Cross was about the same amount as the compensation received in respect of Arnos C. The smaller Arnos B payment from the BDC had been needed to provide other storage facilities for Varma paper and represented no significant element of profit. However when Arnos C closed, Tom Granby found its own accommodation at Avonmouth, with none of the expense of that move falling on Langdons, although Langdons were still entitled to compensation to replace the facility they had lost. The timing could not have been better.

In February 1994, the conversion of the new chilled store and sub-zero facility at Walford Cross was ready. In March Gerber started shipping all its chilled juice from the production line direct to Walford Cross for storage, picking and delivery. In 1995 Langdons extended the chilled store, and in 1996 it built a new store with eight loading bays adjacent to the existing stores. By this time Lloyds Bank was once more happy to provide long-term finance, although, when it jibbed at the cost of the racking, Michael Donoghue and WMAS again came to the rescue with unsecured loans.

If stopping the losses in Arnos B was one turning point for Langdons, converting the warehouse at Walford Cross for Gerber Foods, which took the firm into integrated chilled storage and distribution, was even more significant. Before long a Langdons' lorry would be calling at every Regional Distribution Centre (RDC) of every supermarket in the United Kingdom every day except Christmas and Easter Sunday. Orders for the next day's deliveries would be routed direct to Langdons where a team trained by Paul Rowe and originally working from a Portakabin guaranteed delivery anywhere within 24 hours, with all stock being correctly picked to ensure compliance with use-by dates. No longer was the firm selling just 'wheels' or 'space'. When soon afterwards Michael Donoghue negotiated the sale of the other Bristol lease in Whitby Road, Langdons was at last clear of the losses and problems in Bristol.

Nineteen

WHY NOT EVERYONE THINKS OUR POLICE ARE WONDERFUL

On 18 September 1989 I went to Salisbury to attend with my friend and banker Peter Dobbs, who was retiring as the Regional Manager and Director of Lloyds Bank, a lunch at which various other people in business in the south-west of England were present. Apart from his support for Langdons which I have written about, Peter Dobbs and I had worked together on other occasions, some of which differed from the normal relationship between a banker and his customer. We had gone informally, he in his Porsche and me in my Rover, to look at situations where, although the bank had provided loans, Peter was not entirely sure that the management was telling him the whole truth. I was, at his request, working on the board of a conglomerate to which the bank had lent rather more money than was prudent. In another case, when my involvement in a quoted company at the request of the Welsh Development Agency had been shortly followed by the Midland Bank demanding immediate repayment of its loans, Peter had stepped in to enable the firm to be nursed back to health. When bankers in Ireland had declined to support a telecommunication firm because of its inability to give the kind of security they asked for, Peter had granted an unsecured loan for working capital amounting to £300,000, which had enabled it to become eventually a *succès fou*, an Irish phenomenon, although its English financial support and the nationality of its Chairman were never given undue prominence. (Indeed the Chairman was asked to keep away when Irish officials arranged for the British Ambassador to visit the plant to see how good the Irish were at this kind of thing. At least it saved me a trip.) When inevitably one of our ventures had gone wrong, there had been no recrimination but, on the contrary, a robust defence of the efforts he thought I had made to save the situation.

I was pleased that I had been asked by my companions to speak for all of us in proposing the toast to Peter because, unusually, every word I uttered in his praise as a shrewd banker, an honourable man and a thoroughly nice person was true. After a brief visit to a store to buy a gift for my wife, I made my way to the adjoining car park. As I approached my car, another raced into the same area and came to a screeching halt. Two youths jumped out, vaulted a low wall dividing the car park from a stream, waded along its bed among the discarded supermarket trolleys for a few yards, and then made off into the town. I attempted to follow them but as that involved crossing the stream by a bridge, by the time I was on their side of the water, they had got away.

My impression was that there had been other people around but, apart from a lady whom they had narrowly avoided running over, only the car-park attendant showed any interest in the episode. I asked him to summon the police and, when they arrived, suggested they visit the railway station or local pubs looking out for two young men with trousers wet up to their knees. Later that evening at my home near Taunton I was told by the Salisbury police that the villains had been arrested in a bar and were found to have stolen £700 of goods from the store which I had been visiting. The officer asked me to attend an identity parade at the Salisbury police station the next morning at eleven o'clock.

Having changed my schedule, I drove back to Salisbury. When I arrived, I was not too happy to learn that, due to the pressure on the resources of the Wiltshire Constabulary, no officer was available to see me or to conduct the parade. Indeed such were the constraints under which the guardians of the law were operating that they had not even been able to spare the minute it would have taken them to advise me that my round trip of 120 miles or so would be fruitless. I was invited subsequently to make another visit to Salisbury to make a statement but, as I had already made one, I was unwilling to trespass further on the time of such hard-pressed officers of the law. In due course the miscreants pleaded guilty and were no doubt given a slap on the wrist by the magistrates and their fare back to Bristol out of the Poor Box. The dangerous driving seems to have been overlooked.

On 9 June 1993 a driver called Woolard, who had been an employee of Langdons for only three days, was involved in a minor accident near Warminster in Wiltshire. His traffic operator, Pip Woodman, had asked him before he left Poole if he had enough hours to reach Bristol after something of a mix-up, and he assured her he had. The hours drivers are allowed to work are subject to strict legal regulation, as are the incidence and length of rest periods. When Mr. Woolard had his accident, we can presume he had exceeded the permitted hours, although the evidence in the form of a tachograph from his cab was retained by the police. The officer attending the incident was a constable from the Wiltshire police called Elsbury. As a result of what Woolard told him, or what PC Elsbury inferred from what Woolard told him, the Wiltshire police demanded delivery of all Langdons' tachographs for a prior period of three months. As many of these same records had already been inspected by the officials of the Ministry of Transport under a routine check, there, it might have been thought, the matter might have rested. Mr. Woolard was not retained as a Langdons' driver and left the company in July 1993.

Tachographs, for those who are unfamiliar with the transport industry, provide records of the movement of the vehicle to which they are attached. It is illegal to operate a Heavy Goods Vehicles on a public highway unless the tachograph is recording its movement. A driver who wishes to exceed his permitted hours at the wheel without leaving a record may disconnect the tachograph, either by removing a fuse or by seeking to by-pass it electrically, which is known as 'wiring'. Because of the severe implications of breaking the law over tachographs, which may involve the loss of their operators' licence, transport companies issue clear written instructions to drivers about their use, give them detailed training, and discipline drivers for minor infringements. For the deliberate falsification of a tachograph any Langdons' driver was and is summarily dismissed. The company also has tachographs routinely checked by an outside contractor to ensure that there are no deliberate infringements and to enquire into any minor discrepancies.

It is nonetheless understood by the officials of the Ministry of Transport and generally that there are occasions when a driver cannot avoid breaking the law. He may, for example, find himself in a traffic jam on the motorway and be obliged to stay at the wheel until he can take his vehicle to a place where he is allowed to park. More often, he may take a load of perishable goods to a customer's premises, or call to pick up such a load, and be delayed there because the customer cannot make a loading dock available or because the entire load is not ready for collection, as we saw happening at Gerber Foods. If the customer has a parking area within the compound to which the driver can take his vehicle after it has been loaded or unloaded, there need be no technical breach of the law, unless he is considered to have started working in a rest period. More often, the driver will be made to leave the premises and seek a parking area after a short journey on the highway. In so doing, he may be either driving when he should be resting, or interrupting a long rest period for a matter of minutes while he moves the vehicle. The option which is not available to him, or to his employer, is to refuse to move from the ramp, unless he and they wish to go out of business.

Where such circumstances arise, the firm is unofficially advised by the Ministry officials that the driver should insert his tachograph card but record the exceptional circumstances on the back. It is generally recognised that up to one in twenty cards, each covering a period of a day, can be expected to show a minor infringement. Each such infringement is technically a criminal offence except where a driver is moving on to or off a ferry.

After the tachographs had been in the possession of the Wiltshire Constabulary for several weeks, PC Elsbury called at Walford Cross and asked if he could 'have a chat with' three of Langdons' employees. He was asked if he intended to take statements, in which case a member of the company or a solicitor should be present. He inferred that this was not his intention, although it appears that he was misunderstood or that he changed his mind between Michael Donoghue's office and the Traffic Office, where the 'chats' took place.

Having taken a proof of evidence from one of the drivers myself, I am familiar with the way an interview between an officer from the Wiltshire Constabulary and a driver might have been conducted. In the case which I handled, the officer had been thought-ful enough to let the driver know that he might be fined up to £2,000 or imprisoned for the offences which were being investigated, although that fate might not befall those who were able to assist the police. By that time the police knew the numbers of the drivers' mobile telephones and in this case PC Elsbury had telephoned and interrogated the driver in his cab: this might, if done by a member of the public, have been considered an unsafe procedure, making the person originating the call an accessory to the offence of Driving without Due Care and Attention. PC Elsbury was anxious that the driver should not retain the services of the company's solicitor and that they should meet in Wiltshire rather than in Somerset, no doubt to avoid wasting public funds and police time by his having to travel to the area in which the company was based, and where it might more readily be able to offer help and advice to the driver. He also asked to see correspondence between the driver and Langdons.

On 13 October 1993, 12 police officers, one from the Avon and Somerset force, one from the Wiltshire CID and 10 others from Wiltshire, arrived at Walford Cross in Somerset with a warrant to seize Langdons' documents, including files and computer disks. Initially PC Elsbury, who appeared to be orchestrating matters, refused permission for the company to copy any of the documents before they were removed, the effect of which would have been to have brought its operations to a virtual halt. Fortunately this decision was overruled by a sergeant. Apart from documents concerning traffic, wages and the garage, the police paid particular attention to those in Rob Swindells' office as Commercial Director, from which confidential commercial files and computer disks were taken.

Michael Donoghue was naturally anxious to discover what major criminality the Wiltshire police thought they had uncovered in Langdons so that immediate steps might be taken to stop it. During the raid, most questions about this were ignored. A police sergeant said that Langdons were guilty of 'profiteering', a remark he would have been less confident in making had he seen the filed Statutory Accounts which showed that the company's financial ratios were in line with industry averages. A constable—not PC Elsbury—said they were not looking for tachograph offences. Another remarked that, if all tachographs were perfect, they knew there had to be a fiddle somewhere. No further information was forthcoming before the raiding force departed with its sacks of documents.

In the international transport industry, there is always the possibility of smuggling, and especially the import of illegal drugs, animals or immigrants. Rogue firms substitute prime movers and trailers to pass Ministry of Transport tests, or run 'ghost' vehicles, duplicating identification plates. Others use uncertificated drivers or unplated vehicles. A company carrying high-value goods especially has constantly to operate checks to prevent theft, often in collusion with warehousemen. On top of their other duties, traffic operators must always check drivers' hours through comparing tachographs with other records of journeys, and discipline offenders. Pallet control is another area where systematic dishonesty can occur.

In the weeks which followed the raid, there was no intimation of what the Wiltshire police were so concerned about as to be devoting substantial resources to investigating a firm in another district operating without major customers in their area. It was not until 12 April 1994, 10 months after Mr. Woolard had been questioned, that the Chief Constable, Walter Girven, told me that the operation was being conducted under the supervision of Superintendent Toynton and that 120 offences relating to tachograph charts were being investigated. As over 3,200 charts had been removed during the raid, that figure fell comfortably within the 5 per cent of the total which the Ministry of Transport acknowledges may show a technical infringement without any criminal intent.

In the weeks following the raid, officers from Wiltshire, sometimes in a party of four, visited Langdons' customers or the depots which Langdons' vehicles visited up and down the country to check when vehicles had moved into or out of the premises, or to view security videos. This information was then correlated with the tachographs of individual drivers. A parallel investigation involved comparing the wage sheets of individual drivers with their tachographs to see how many more 'working' hours they had been paid than those during which they were recorded on the tachograph as having driven. If the seizure of records had been highly inconvenient, the visits to customers were in some cases highly damaging. Those who telephoned to say 'We hear you've got the Fraud Squad in' could at least be told the position. Others didn't phone and one of them at least decided not to renew a major contract without explanation.

Throughout this difficult time, it would seem that only two drivers, both having left the company somewhat disaffected, told the police something along the lines of what they wanted or expected to hear, which was that undue pressure had been put on them to achieve unrealistic delivery targets. Other drivers reported being asked plaintively, 'Why are you so loyal to Langdons?' What they did was to tell the truth, which was that, although traffic operators wanted their drivers to keep to delivery slots agreed with customers, they did not encourage the drivers to break the law and disciplined them if they were found doing so. Among the records in which the police seemed to take no interest were those from the hubometers, by which the firm ran an extra covert check on the mileage of vehicles to ensure that there was no running without tachographs. They might also have seen from the computer data on each tractor's fuel consumption which was prepared and monitored weekly that this too was a check to prevent illegal running: any trips made without the tachograph immediately show as a variant in the anticipated mileage per gallon and lead to an investigation.

Charges for certain non-indictable offences, including those involving non-fraudulent misuse of tachographs, have to be brought within six months of information being laid before the Court. On 26 April 1994, just within the six-month deadline, summonses were issued against Langdons and 12 drivers alleging tachograph offences, to be heard in a Magistrates' Court in Wiltshire in June. With the exception of the summons against Mr. Woolard, all the offences were alleged to have taken place in Wiltshire or elsewhere, and were clearly bad in law, hastily issued, and spattered with Tippex. As expected, they were withdrawn on 8 June before the hearing, with costs of £2,217.93 being awarded to the defendants.

The influential trade paper, *Commercial Motor*, in its issue dated 19-25 May 1994 ran an article referring to this impending prosecution of Langdons and 10 of its staff. While it is normal for a trade paper to publish the result of proceedings, it is unusual for it to become aware of, let alone publish, details of summonses. It is of course possible that the reporters working for the *Commercial Motor* visit every Magistrates' Court in the country every day on the off chance that a haulage company or a driver has had a summons issued against it or him. Another possibility is that someone tipped them off, with a view to performing a public service by warning the world that Langdons might be engaging in criminal activities. Taken in conjunction with the police visits to customers, the effect of the article was to throw further mud in the direction of Walford Cross.

In his letter to me of 12 April 1994 Mr. Girvan had told me that the Crown Prosecution Service (CPS) was involved in the case. For my American reader(s), I must explain that the CPS performs much of the functions of a District Attorney, but without being responsible to the electorate. Before it was formed, police officers conducted prosecutions in minor cases, often forming a close working relationship with defence solicitors. In more serious cases, local advocates would be instructed to act on behalf of the prosecution. This system had the advantage that an advocate gained the experience of appearing from time to time for either side—prosecution or defence, poacher or gamekeeper. This led to a better administration of justice because advocates learned that winning at any cost was not the issue. Many lawyers and Chief Constables saw the establishment of the CPS as a retrograde step, not least because, apart from breeding a culture where winning becomes more important than justice, it might attract only those lawyers not confident or able enough to make a career in private practice. That of course is not what happened in Wiltshire.

The months passed. Although it appeared that the Wiltshire police had been interested only in the drivers of temperature-controlled vehicles where a driver usually stays with his trailer, they decided to widen the investigation by taking from the Lafarge plasterboard plant at Avonmouth all records of vehicles entering and leaving the premises during January 1995. With ambient trailers, which are less costly than those subject to temperature control, it is normal for a driver to drop one trailer for loading and leave at once with another already loaded. In this way he loses no time waiting for his load to be tipped or loaded. Having taken the records from Lafarge, the Wiltshire police sent again for Langdons' tachographs. Neither the Avon and Somerset Constabulary (in whose area Avonmouth lies), nor the Ministry of Transport, which has primary responsibility for enforcement of driving regulations, appear to have taken part in this exercise. Lafarge seems to have been chosen because it was one of Langdons' biggest customers. Other reports continued to come in of further enquiries by PC Elsbury and his colleagues, including news of police officers in two other areas who stopped vehicles, telling the drivers that the Wiltshire police had warned them to keep an eye on Langdons.

It emerged eventually that there had been three matters which continued to concern the Wiltshire police, none of which had any connection with Wiltshire. The first was that drivers had been paid by Langdons while they were resting as well as while they were driving, on the basis that an employee stranded on a ramp in Doncaster cannot slip back home to Taunton for a cup of tea. The police formed the view that, as the drivers were being paid, they cannot have been resting. Fortunately that interpretation was not one with which Leading Counsel and legal precedent is in agreement, nor was it likely to appeal to a jury.

The second issue concerned whether a driver was or was not working while the vehicle was being loaded or unloaded by third parties. Again, the police view appeared to have been formed in the days when drivers were expected to assist in these processes, before loading-docks and fork-lifts and pallets. Today, with temperature-controlled traffic especially, drivers are never allowed to get involved.

On the third issue, certain Langdons' drivers were technically at fault. When they had to move a vehicle on to or off a ramp, they should have entered their tachograph and noted the request to move. Some did, but others drove for a short distance without inserting the tachograph. What they did was what is standard throughout the industry: how they did it was technically wrong. The majority of infringements appeared to arise from visits to Pura Foods in London to pick up loads, where there was a record of long delays, and no parking area on the site to which a driver could move a vehicle when the loading was complete and he was told to leave the ramp. Others arose from delays waiting for a load at Gerber Foods in Bridgwater.

Offences by individual drivers were inevitably uncovered. One at least had stolen a 'dodgy night': driving home with her tachograph removed and then back to the place where the rest should have been taken. Another had inexplicably driven 15 miles between Taunton and Chard without inserting a tachograph. A third had not used a tachograph at all, but he was a shunter who never went on the public highway. A fourth turned out to be not a regular driver, but a fitter in the garage whose brother (with the same surname) was a driver. An unrecorded journey from Teesside to Taunton which caused great excitement turned out to have been made on a low-loader after a breakdown. And so on. With thousands of cards and hundreds of time-sheets, some drivers had cheated over the hours of work they claimed and some had technically broken the law. The police had been able to find this out because they had the power and resource to visit Langdons' customers and delivery points, and demand to see records. But there was no evidence that traffic operators, and especially Christopher Murt and Rupert Ryall, had done more than try to provide the best service to customers within the constraints under which the industry operates: nor that the firm had at any time been guilty of any kind of impropriety.

On 7 August 1995 a journalist from the *Commercial Motor* spoke to Rob Swindells on the telephone asking him to comment on the fact that Christopher Murt, Rupert Ryall and 20 drivers were to be charged with conspiring to make false tachograph records. A charge of conspiracy is an indictable offence and therefore the six-month limitation on the issue of proceedings would not apply. An article naming Christopher and Rupert appeared in the issue dated 10-16 August 1995, although this issue may not have been available, for some reason or other, until a day later than usual. The summonses had not been not issued until 8 August, at which date they first came into the public domain, and they were not served until 11 and 12 August. The only other people who had knowledge of their preparation and the names of those involved on 7 August, when the journalist called Langdons, were the court officials, the CPS, and the Wiltshire Police. The only party which admitted having spoken to a journalist working for or in touch with the *Commercial Motor* was the Wiltshire Police, whose zeal for good relations with the press may have obscured their recollection of the provisions of the Data Protection Act. Langdons were convinced that the information had been improperly, even maliciously, leaked to the press.

Having had over two years in which to consider their position, the CPS amended the charges two weeks before the hearing in February 1996 so that all the defendants would have to remain in court for the duration of the entire trial. If they pleaded not guilty, as indeed they wished to of conspiracy, Counsel advised that the outcome of the trial would be uncertain because both Christopher Murt and Rupert Ryall were technically guilty of a lesser charge of aiding and abetting drivers in the commission of an offence, in that they knew that on occasion a driver had to move off a ramp when out of hours, or might fail to restart his rest period after such a move. It was of course out-of-time for the CPS to make this the substantive charge, whence the accusation of conspiracy.

A conspiracy charge, as my esteemed tutor in criminal law at Cambridge Henry Barnes taught me, is the last refuge in English law of a desperate prosecutor. It is the charge you bring when all else has failed. And it was the charge which the authorities in Wiltshire came up with in an attempt to justify what had been going on, if they were not prepared to admit their mistake. The police had devoted three years (and many man-years) to sifting through documents and trying unsuccessfully to find un-biased witnesses who would say what they wanted to hear. They had visited supermar-ket depots and food manufactures up and down the country. They had combed though sackfuls of contracts, quotations, time-sheets, expense claims, garage records, disks, and accounts. Their efforts had been unavailing. No wrongdoing had been uncovered apart from routine tachograph offences, and none at all on the part of what seems to have been the main target, Langdons. These police efforts, it should be noted, were made by a force which could not spare an officer to take a single statement at a time of its own choosing in its own police station in a case of robbery and dangerous driving in its own cathedral city. No blame for this waste of resource can be attached to PC Elsbury, who was in fact commended by the Recorder for his efforts. If there was a fault line in the fabric of the Wiltshire Constabulary, it ran right to the top.

On Counsel's advice, and unable to contemplate the damage to the business which would result if Christopher Murt, Rupert Ryall and 20 drivers had to spend upwards of a month in court, the defendant drivers pleaded guilty to certain offences other than conspiracy. Christopher Murt and Rupert Ryall, who were responsible for the traffic operation, pleaded guilty to aiding and abetting the technical offences, which had occurred due to the delays at Gerber and Pura Foods. All the conspiracy charges were dismissed, but they had served their purpose in bringing the defendants to court out of time and so, in some eyes perhaps, justifying the investigation and prosecution. The total amount of the fines on all the defendants amounted to £6,750, a derisory figure in the normal context of tachograph and road traffic offences. Costs of more than £14,000 were requested by the prosecution and they were awarded £1,750, or £467.93 less than Langdons had been given in respect of the dismissal of the earlier summonses.

The cost of the affair to Langdons in wasted management time and lost business cannot be calculated. The legal fees for the defence amounted to around £55,000, of which £50,000 was covered by insurance against precisely this kind of action. How much time and money the police spent on their enquiries, and how much crime in Wiltshire went undetected as a result, will never be known.

Although in these proceedings the company had not been charged with, let alone found guilty of, any offence, the convictions of its employees meant that Langdons had to make a special appearance before the Traffic Commissioners where, if it had been in the wrong, new operating licences might have been refused or existing ones withdrawn. After hearing all the facts and recognising the technical nature of the offences, the Commissioner commented on the need to comply with the law in all respects and proceeded to award the firm an additional 10 operating licences.

The lessons for a haulier? Pay your drivers a weekly wage, and not hourly, so that people who don't understand the business aren't misled by the fact that the figures differ from those on the tachographs. If a driver has to move the vehicle under exceptional circumstances, make sure he notes the details on the tachograph. And don't let your employees become inveigled into any 'chats' with police officers.

The Crown Prosecution Service too, under its leader (Dame) Barbara Mills, has been found to be no less free of blemish than other organisations operating in the public sector. On taking over the leading role from the Dame, David Calvert-Smith had threatened to dismiss incompetent lawyers in an effort to restore public confidence in the CPS, reporting that some of the staff were 'beyond redemption'. On 21 July 1999 he too admitted defeat, saying, 'No lawyer or any other member of the staff has been asked to go simply because of their incompetence. There is quite a bureaucratic scheme within the Civil Service as to what you can and cannot do with your employees. The process whereby lawyers, or anyone else can simply be got rid of for incompetence is extremely complicated.'

And the lessons for the Wiltshire Constabulary and the ratepayers of that fortunate county? Maybe they should have learned something, from the token size of the fines imposed by the Recorder, the amount of costs which he awarded, and the attitude of the Traffic Commissioner. Mr. Girven is now retired and it might have been hoped that his lady successor might, while sharing his interest in the relentless pursuit of criminals, nevertheless choose to allocate her scant resources with better judgment and closer to home.

Unfortunately, such hopes have yet to be fulfilled. On 2 September 1998 four Langdons' lorries were driving through Wiltshire on the M4 when one of them was stopped at random by PC Elsbury. There is nothing sinister about this: heavy goods vehicles are routinely stopped by the police. The driver, Carl Spink, handed over to PC Elsbury 20 tachograph cards which he had with him in the cab. The cards showed blips where the vehicle had been moved a short distance without the cards having been inserted, in two cases less than a mile and in the third perhaps two miles. These discrepancies would have been picked up by Langdons' external card monitor, and Mr. Spink would in due course have been disciplined by the firm.

Ignoring the trivial nature of the possible offences and the fact that they had not been committed in Wiltshire, the police, as before, made visits outside the county to check the times at which Mr. Spink had booked into and out of various depots. It transpired that he had indeed been asked to move his vehicle in or from customers' premises and, contrary to his instructions, had not inserted a card and written on the back why he had moved. Although there was no suggestion of Mr. Spink having worked in a rest period, PC Elsbury in his evidence to the court went to some lengths to explain the purpose of overnight rest breaks.

The case was set down for hearing at Chippenham in Wiltshire on 27 July 1999, some ten months after the driver had been stopped. The CPS failed to disclose its evidence to the defence in due time, causing an adjournment until 24 August 1999. The justices took the view that the discrepancies were minor but because Mr. Spink is a professional driver and should have known better, they fined him £50 on each charge, with £45 costs.

It would be again a mistake to suggest that the enthusiastic PC Elsbury, still on road traffic duties, was to blame for this further expenditure of police time and public money. Police constables do not go on their travels to remote parts of the kingdom when they are off duty, or without the knowledge and backing of their superiors. The new Chief Constable may care to ask whether the exercise involving Carl Spink would have been sanctioned if he had not worked for Langdons; and how many other fishing expeditions her officers go on in preference to policing their own patch.

Twenty

WHY TAUNTON CIDER STOPPED BEING
CIDER FROM TAUNTON

You will recall from Chapter Seventeen the sequence of events which led to Taunton Cider Ltd being bought by its management with the aid of City financiers, becoming a public company soon afterwards. It had then been taken over by Matthew Clark, which already owned other well-known cider brands, for around £275 million. The decision of the Taunton board to negotiate with Matthew Clark for the sale of Taunton Cider was not taken simply so that those who had taken up shares in the management buy-out could become richer, or without considering what options were open for the firm if it continued trading independently. A factor had to be the charismatic figure of Peter Aikens who, in a very few years, had with his skilful acquisitions brought Matthew Clark from the comparative obscurity of a drinks wholesaler into the big league as a national manufacturer. Mr. Aikens had first won his spurs as Production Director of Courage and his skills as a production engineer were shown to good effect when it came to rationalising the rambling Showerings empire, concentrating the cider production in Shepton Mallet and closing other plants. When he first started talking to the Taunton board about a bid in September 1995, his reputation could not have been higher. As one of those involved put it, 'He seemed as if he could walk on water'. That was fine, so long as he didn't think so himself.

Taunton Cider's management had recognised many of the problems even before Brian Longstaff left in 1993. The site at Norton Fitzwarren was hemmed in by houses. Every planning application led to objections from a few local householders. The situation was not improved by a planning officer who tipped residents off about preliminary discussions between the company and the Borough Council, no doubt with the public-spirited and laudable intention of giving them plenty of time in which to organise their unfailing opposition. Because of the space restrictions, canning of cider had been sub-contracted to Hall and Woodhouse, in far-away Blandford, which involved tankers taking down the cider and curtain-sided trailers bringing back the cans. To supplement the bottling capacity, Taunton Cider had leased facilities at the Whitbread brewery in Tiverton, again involving expensive fetching and carrying.

In 1993 the management at Norton Fitzwarren devised a scheme to resolve the space restriction. The company bought some 23 acres of land from Mr. Underhill, a neighbouring farmer, with the ultimate intention of relocating the entire operation away from any private houses. The scheme also involved a bypass for the village of Norton Fitzwarren and a bridge over the notorious level crossing at Silk Mills, where queues of traffic wait every few minutes for the passing of trains between Taunton and Exeter. This level crossing was only a part of the traffic problem: it frequently took as long as 30 minutes for a lorry to reach the M5 motorway which ran the other side of Taunton. In transport terms, the factory was in the wrong place.

Then there was the fear that cider sales had peaked, coupled with the robust and successful defence Bulmers mounted of their dominant market position, which involved the lowering of prices and therefore of margins and profits. The Taunton board tried three diversifications away from cider. We have already looked at the flavoured water

111

called *Piermont*, and at the pressed apple-juice marketed under the name *Copella*, which never really challenged *Appletise* and, one way and another, involved a loss of over £6 million by the time it was sold back to the people from whom it had originally been bought. The third venture was the agency for the distribution of the American *Millers Genuine Draft* beer. This agreement for three years spanned the Matthew Clark purchase and was not renewed.

The Board of Taunton Cider considered two moves of more significance which might have strengthened its position by removing dependence on a single product. The first we have already mentioned—the acquisition of Showerings. The second was the purchase of Britvic, in which Bass still held a 30 per cent stake; with the close Bass relationship and the brewer seeming to lose interest in peripheral activities, this looked the better option. Exercises were done, consultants retained and remunerated, meetings were held, but no decisions were made and neither option was taken.

Another worry was the threat from the competition, and especially from Bulmers. The five-year supply agreements with former shareholders were drawing to a close. Bass, the biggest customer, was making ominous noises about dual-sourcing in future, with Bulmers as the other supplier. The nightmare was that cider would come to be regarded as no more than a commodity, when imports would eat into the market share of the domestic producers, without their makers having to incur the expense of national advertising. The very threat of supermarkets and other retailers looking abroad for supply was enough to drive down prices and give the management sleepless nights.

These then were among the considerations which affected the decision of the Taunton Board in its discussions with Peter Aikens, who seemed in many respects to be planning to do no more than they had themselves considered. In the preliminary discussions all the key Taunton managers—Peter Adams, Nick Pearch, Andy Nash, Neil Rixon and Colin Todd—expected to remain with the company to ease the transition and help build the new business. Inevitably, someone who has been number one may not relish demotion to a subsidiary position. Peter Adams, as we saw, left Taunton when the sale was completed. Nick Pearch stayed for two meetings of the committee set up under Peter Aikens's chairmanship to oversee the integration of Taunton Cider into Matthew Clark and then decided to leave. Andy Nash and Neil Rixon lasted a little longer.

We last talked about Neil Rixon when he was in negotiation with Michael Donoghue for Langdons to take over the warehousing and distribution of the entire output of Taunton Cider. By the autumn of 1995 all the detailed work had been completed. Prices for the equipment to be sold had been agreed. Transfers of engagements for the staff involved had been arranged. All that was missing was a decision on the cut-off date. Then, when he became privy to the negotiations with Matthew Clark, Neil Rixon had to play for time, being unable to explain to Langdons what was happening any more than Peter Adams could when he had met Michael Donoghue on the plane. As soon as the sale to Matthew Clark was completed, Neil was confirmed as Logistics Director. He was told that the plan was to end the distribution of cider from Norton Fitzwarren as soon as possible, concentrating all deliveries from a new warehouse to be built on the outskirts of Bristol. In the meanwhile Matthew Clark had entered into a contract with a Bristol firm called Pearsons to rent a warehouse at Hartcliffe in Bristol for a period of 15 months while the new facility was being built.

The need to give statutory notice of redundancy to the personnel in Norton Fitzwarren meant that the changeover had to be delayed until March 1996. During these three months Langdons continued to hope that they would remain the lead haulier for Taunton Cider, albeit operating from Hartcliffe rather than closer to home. Efforts to arrange meetings with Matthew Clark at a decision-making level proved unavailing, perhaps because those involved felt they had more important matters to sort out. Neil Rixon did what he could to provide assurances about the continuing involvement of Langdons, but the responsibility for making those decisions no longer rested in his hands, for all his title and apparent authority. The plan for immediately concentrating the dispatches in Bristol had been adopted without his opinion being sought. The decision had possibly been taken on the advice of, and certainly was enthusiastically supported by, consultants retained by Matthew Clark, whose staff was strengthened by the presence of Peter Aikens's son, Michael. The influence of the consultants, and the immutability of the plans, was evidenced by their presence at every weekly meeting of the Integration Committee.

Although only the warehousing contract at Hartcliffe had been given to Pearsons, they had also expected a contract in parallel for the haulage. As their transport experience was largely for a customer called Brabantia, which was not in the drinks trade, it might have seemed unreasonable as well as unwise to entrust them with the Taunton Cider distribution. Matthew Clark already used the substantial firm BOC for much of its work, but, although BOC were familiar with the exigencies of the drinks trade, they too had not been awarded the Taunton Cider haulage contract. Neil Rixon therefore found himself expected to operate from a site which was difficult to work, using a scheduler who was unfamiliar with the business, depending on equally unfamiliar warehousemen, some fifty miles from the factory, with no haulier having been given a contract to provide the transport facilities.

When the cut-off day arrived, Langdons located seven standing trailers at Hartcliffe to facilitate loading, despite not having received the contract which they thought they had been promised. Predicting a disaster if the distribution pattern adopted were not to be changed and wishing to continue to take advantage of Langdons' experience in working for Taunton Cider, Neil Rixon started pressing for reconsideration of the arrangement whereby Pearsons did the scheduling and could cherry-pick the transport work, in addition to the warehousing. He was then taken aside by one of Matthew Clark's consultants and warned against persisting with his criticism. A week later he was made redundant.

The transfer of dispatch to Hartcliffe would have been difficult enough even with Langdons running it. Their offer to locate at Hartcliffe Steve Dare and Dorothy Brown, the Langdons' employees who were most familiar with the Taunton Cider distribution

Dorothy Brown.

pattern, was turned down, possibly by George Pearson himself, who may have thought he could handle the job without involving a competitor. Even at no charge for the Langdons' staff located at Hartcliffe, Pearsons were not prepared to make an office available for them so that the scheduling of deliveries could be improved, and the paperwork tightened up. The presence of Steve and Dorothy, both extremely experienced operators, who were both willing to work in Bristol, might have helped to prevent at least some of the muddle which was soon to develop. It was not Matthew Clark's concern that Langdons' trailers tended to be the last to be loaded and their drivers given the less profitable work, so long as the correct product was being made, shunted, marshalled and delivered to customers; but it wasn't. To do that you need experienced traffic operators, good back-up in paperwork, an efficient warehouse, close production control and planning, adequate transport equipment and an efficient IT system. When loads were rejected by customers because of wrong picking in the Hartcliffe warehouse, shortages, incorrect paperwork, late delivery and the like, the Matthew Clark staff there seemed unable to comprehend the commercial implications of their failures.

Like most firms in the 1990s, Taunton Cider's Information Technology began to creak as the business expanded and the technology developed. In early 1995 the firm started to replace an aggregation of customised software with the comprehensive SAP R3 protocol, which embraces everything from procurement through manufacture and finance to order capture and dispatch. By the time of the takeover in November, production planning and material sourcing were on SAP but order capture and warehouse management remained on the old systems. Matthew Clark decided to replace the warehouse management systems with OPUS as used in its northern warehouse at Worksop, and to do so simultaneously with the switch of warehousing and dispatch to Hartcliffe. This gave what must have been inadequate time to test OPUS on the changeover and to ensure that it was capable of immediately replacing the Taunton systems already in place. So far as warehousing and dispatch went, there was no running in parallel. If OPUS did not immediately provide the information to manage order capture, resupply and delivery, the service to customer would fall below an acceptable level. And that is what happened, on top of all the other obstacles which had been thrown in the logistical path. The public announcements of the Matthew Clark board, seeking to explain away the poor performance of Taunton Cider, were later to speak only of Alcopops and foreign imports. There were other factors.

Neil Rixon was replaced as Logistics Director responsible for the distribution of Taunton Cider by Martin Grisman, another able and fair operator who was an ex-Taunton Cider employee, although he was no more in a position to circumvent the obstacles arising from the precipitate move to Hartcliffe and the IT problems than his predecessor had been. Despite the difficulties inherent in the Hartcliffe operation and the growing dissatisfaction of customers with the poor service they were receiving, the volume of Langdons' business kept up well until August 1996, when the amount billed fell to £103,300 against £140,200 the previous year. Some of the drop in turnover was due to the traffic being carried by Pearsons and other sub-contractors. More ominous was the fact that, despite it being summer and the height of the drinking season, demand for Taunton Cider products was falling, with Sainsbury's in particular expressing dissatisfaction over poor service.

Another cause of Langdons' lost business with Matthew Clark, and possibly for further inefficiency, was that if the staff at Hartcliffe saw a sub-contractor working for Langdons, they were prepared to go direct to the sub-contractor for quotations for future work. In the road-transport industry, every main contractor uses sub-contractors to smooth periods of excessive demand, aiming to make not less than 10 per cent to cover administration and finance costs. The main contractor is expected to find vehicles for whatever needs shifting at short notice, and hold equipment so that he can meet such expectations. The sub-contractor typically runs with low overheads, picking and choosing his work. One runs a scheduled bus service, the other a taxi. A customer is usually unwise to try to bypass the main contractor in pursuit of short-term gain because he will soon find himself without transport during a rush period. That is what Matthew Clark did, and that is what almost certainly happened.

The fall in sales may also have been attributed in part to the cuts in certain of the Taunton Cider budgets under Matthew Clark's ownership. We have noted earlier how large a portion of the Taunton budget had been devoted to sales and marketing, ensuring that the more profitable premium brands held their shares and it is possible that some of the money spent on television advertising had been wasteful and excessive. The number of people involved in the commercial side amounted to two thirds of those engaged in production and it would not be surprising that someone needing to make economies and coming from a production background might have decided that the selling costs were too high and chosen this area in particular for retrenchment. At all events, it seems that, to cut costs, advertising was reduced and sales and marketing people lost their jobs. To compound the difficulties, Matthew Clark could not, as the independent company had done, rely on the marketing flair of Peter Adams, and before long it was to lose the equally experienced Andy Nash.

Throughout the autumn of 1996, Langdons' share of the shuttle from Norton Fitzwarren and the deliveries from Hartcliffe continued to fall. Steve Dare withdrew the standing trailers as the business dropped away. Even December, traditionally a bumper month for drink sales, saw no arresting of the decline. A new problems arose when Pearsons decided that, as the warehouse was bonded, they would no longer allow a Langdons' driver to check his load before leaving, having to sign for it unseen. Often these loads were wrongly marshalled, leading to shortages, overages, cross-overs and all the other horrors occasionally inherent in running a good warehouse and endemic in a bad one. At times the Matthew Clark staff refused to accept returns at Hartcliffe, nor was it permitted for the haulier to take back the rejects back to the factory at Norton Fitzwarren. Langdons solved the dilemma by storing these returned and rejected goods in the trusty Unit 13 at the former SRD, where pallet after pallet, case upon case, of returned cider accumulated. For months Langdons could get no decision out of Matthew Clark about this stock until finally, when it was all over, they returned the lot to the factory in Norton Fitzwarren so that at least the Excise Duty could be reclaimed.

At the end of January 1997 Michael Donoghue sent a plea to Martin Grisman asking for some guidance as to what might be expected of Langdons in the future. Having given details of the fall in revenue, he asked 'What have Langdons done wrong?'. On 19 February Martin replied that Matthew Clark were in the process of reviewing their transport arrangements for the coming year, and that Langdons would be part of that. On 20 March Langdons' drivers made two late deliveries and immediately the firm was refused further business out of Hartcliffe, although, when Rob

Swindells explained the circumstances, Alan Trent of Matthew Clark told him that normal business relations would be resumed the following week. For a month after that neither of the Matthew Clark people responsible at Hartcliffe, Alan Trent and Bridget McCann, was prepared to talk to anyone in Langdons, nor were Langdons' vehicles given any work.

Although there had been no complaint about their service apart from the two late deliveries, Matthew Clark stopped paying Langdons money which was owed and about which there was no dispute, including £18,632.51 in respect of February invoices. On 27 May 1997 Langdons issued a summons claiming £33,353.56 plus interest, court fees and costs, from which was deducted £8,660.64 in respect of what Langdons owed Matthew Clark for hiring the former Norton Fitzwarren tractors to do their work. On 6 June Matthew Clark's lawyers wrote agreeing to pay the amounts due plus interest but demurring over the payment of costs. A week later all the sums owing including costs were paid in full.

By February 1997 Langdons had already decided that they could not continue with Matthew Clark as a principal customer. On 25 March I watched with Michael Donoghue as eight tractors and 28 trailers were auctioned at the SRD in Norton Fitzwarren. Many other tractors and trailers had already been sold and on that day alone the company received a cheque from the auctioneers of £284,000 plus VAT, of which some £80,000 went to pay off outstanding hire-purchase commitments. Michael Donoghue estimated that the take-over of Taunton Cider by Matthew Clark and the subsequent efforts to work for them had involved Langdons losing around £160,000. Happily the number of redundancies was few, and none of the drivers involved was out of work for long. The profit on the sale of the equipment was also in the region of £160,000, as many of the trailers had been fully depreciated. If they had been on contract hire, the story would have been different.

The loss of the Taunton Cider work which could not be replaced with locally generated business and the unfortunate experience at Hartcliffe persuaded the Langdons' board that the company's future lay in concentrating on temperature-controlled operations. For whatever reason, Pearsons subsequently curtailed their transport operations, although they remain in the warehousing business.

Matthew Clark, faced with losses of turnover, decided to close the Norton Fitzwarren factory and move all manufacture to the Showerings plant at Shepton Mallet, although this was a rational decision which may have been in the master-plan when the takeover took place in November 1995. Peter Aikens was also subjected to relocation at Shepton Mallet, although the cost of the move to him personally was alleviated by a payment somewhere in excess of £400,000 on behalf of the shareholders of Matthew Clark, a sum to which sections of the press and the City seemed to take the most unreasonable exception.

In November 1998, three years after the takeover of Taunton Cider plc, the shareholders in Matthew Clark received a document from their Chairman, Graham Wilson. He told them of significant challenges which had had to be faced, of the rapid rise of alcopops, of the aggressive pricing policy of Bulmers, of the influx of cheap imported drinks and of 'the extremely active management by supermarket stores and cash and carry outlets of their buying margins'. He continued: 'Because of the prevailing market uncertainty over Matthew Clark's share price and the recent series of adverse comments from the alcoholic beverages industry, your board has concluded that Matthew Clark's businesses can more effectively be developed within a larger and more widely based drinks group, with a strong balance sheet able to support the future development of the business'. The Board recommended that shareholders accept 243p per share for their holdings, as he, his Board and their families had already committed to do in respect of the 0.2 per cent which they owned. The net assets of Matthew Clark plc on 30 April 1998 were £95.4 million and the price of the share had dropped to 134p on 21 October 1998 when the company announced the possibility of a bid. The buyer was Canandaigua Ltd, an American-owned firm more interested in drinks distribution than in cider manufacture, it might seem.

And what of those Taunton Cider employees in Norton Fitzwarren? Nearly all of them lost their jobs although many found similar work at Gerber Foods in Bridgwater. The householders who routinely objected to every planning application can sleep more happily in the knowledge that they will one day be surrounded by more houses, although what employment the newcomers will find is as yet an unanswered question.

On 14 July 1999 Bulmers announced that *Strongbow* had increased its annual sales by 9 per cent despite a fall of 3 per cent in cider sales nationally. Its profits had risen in the year by 28 per cent and, although the import of cheap beer imports was mentioned, there was nothing said about alcopops. A comment was made that 'Fears that, under new ownership, Matthew Clark would launch an all-out assault on the industry have proven unfounded'. Bulmers too had closed some factories but they still provide many jobs in and around Hereford. They had not, it seems, tried simultaneously to relocate their main warehouse, introduce a new computer system, cut their sales force, and sideline their reliable and trusty haulier. Making things is one art, selling them another, and efficiently distributing them is a third.

Peter Aikens said later that he had paid too much for Taunton Cider. As things turned out, he and the other members of the Matthew Clark board must have been thankful that they and their families owned no more than one five-hundredth part of the business. In the various financial deals we have noted, some people made money, and others lost it. Ultimately the real losers were the people of Taunton, and especially those who worked in Norton Fitzwarren at Taunton Cider plc.

Twenty-One

How a Chilled Network of Shared-User Traffic Turned into Chillnet

As we have noted so often, merely carrying a full load on a vehicle from one place to another is a fairly simple business, something anyone with an Operator's Licence can do, and so it is likely to be very competitive. The more complications the haulier can add to his task, the less competition will he face and the better and more stable his business will be. Thus temperature-controlled haulage is less competitive than the carriage of dry goods at ambient temperatures because of the need to control and monitor the temperature in the trailer or rigid vehicle and to make a delivery before the goods deteriorate. The temperature-controlled vehicle is more costly, which for the most part keeps cowboys out of the market. Many hauliers offer either a chilled service, at temperatures from +1 degree centigrade to +5, or a sub-zero service at -18 degrees or lower. If you can offer both, especially using the same vehicle, you have a further advantage; but, again, the dual-purpose vehicles are more expensive, again raising the entry barrier.

Another variant is between full loads and part loads. A full load is simple, especially if it is being delivered, or 'dropped' in the parlance, at a single location. The greater the number of drops, the more complex the problems for the driver and his traffic controller, because a delay at any one destination may involve not making later deliveries through missed slots or the driver running out of hours. A haulier who offers facilities for the delivery of less than a full load will either run part-empty, and therefore inefficiently, and charge accordingly, or he needs facilities for consolidation with loads from other customers, what is called in the jargon 'shared user traffic'. Sending a single pallet, or even five pallets, in a vehicle of whatever size anywhere is much more costly than using a trailer which can carry 26 pallets because each vehicle needs only one driver and one prime mover. (A 'prime mover' is a single tractor or rigid vehicle, another bit of jargon.) A haulier who can offer delivery of small numbers of pallets at rates calculated on his ability to consolidate is more competitive than one who lacks the facilities for consolidation.

Another ingredient in the cake is the return-load factor. We have noted earlier the importance of having outward traffic from sources close to the haulier's base. To stay competitive, he needs to aim for not less than 70 per cent loading on his return leg. You may recall that Langdons had to drop the Aaronson's plasterboard business from South Molton after the management buy-out because they were unable to find return traffic into North Devon while the outward traffic was too far from the Taunton base to be economical on a stand-alone basis.

So far we have established a model which, to work efficiently, calls for mixed temperature-controlled sub-zero or chilled traffic in full loads of up to 26 pallets made up as necessary through consolidation with not less than 70 per cent return loads. With chilled or frozen foodstuffs it is not feasible to consolidate loads in an open yard or an unrefrigerated warehouse for reasons of hygiene as well as temperature. The haulier who offers such consolidation must therefore have facilities for collecting small numbers of pallets efficiently and then taking them to a central depot where they can be unloaded—'cross-docked' in the jargon—and held at the right temperature until they can be marshalled in full loads for onward delivery. In addition to the inward and outward carriage, he will be able in effect to charge twice for cross-docking, although it will normally be wrapped up in a single figure, and once for storage and picking. If he can reach agreement with the manufacturer that all the traffic will be immediately shipped to the haulier's warehouse for storage as it comes off the production line, for picking and delivery later rather than being held in the manufacturer's own warehouse, so much the better. The manufacturer will have more space available for production and be able to claim from the haulier if any deliveries are not made: the haulier will have a customer who may find it difficult to change to someone else because of the cost and delay involved in providing another temperature-controlled store.

Temperature-controlled storage at Walford Cross, Taunton in 1998.

Our perfect model also involves making reciprocal arrangements for return traffic. All the facilities for the collection and consolidation of part-loads have to be available at similar hubs to what exists at the haulier's home base or bases. These hubs have to be within a distance from each other to which a driver can make a return journey and unload, and be reloaded, within his permitted hours. Once the hubs are in place, the vehicle carrying a full complement of pallets to another hub—'trunking' in the jargon—can pick up a similar return load from that hub destined for his home base, where it can be cross-docked, sorted and then finally delivered in the smaller vehicles which are going out next day to collect goods from local manufacturers. In the perfect model, all the vehicles are both collecting and delivering in a 24-hour cycle, and the 'trunkers' may be double-manned and double-shifted, so further increasing their revenue.

Trunking is, however, only a minor part of the service which has to be available. Most of the full loads will be destined for the Regional Distribution Centres (RDCs) of the supermarket chains. To offer a scheduled, regular daily service to all comers, the haulier has to be already committed to making daily deliveries to each of the RDCs because it is not possible on an *ad hoc* basis merely to turn up with three or four pallets from time to time and expect to be unloaded (or 'tipped' in the argot). He also has to have similar commitments to other wholesalers such as Booker, Mace, Spar and so on; and the other hubs have also to be able to offer the same service to customers within their local distribution area as he is offering from his own base.

The final piece of the model relates to Information Technology. In the optimum solution, the orders from the customers are also sent direct to the haulier for assembly, cross-docking, storage, picking and dispatch with self-billing on a daily basis. A company offering this service has to be not just totally committed to using the latest software and equipment, but every member of staff concerned in the operation has to be computer-numerate. Consider for a moment the factors to be taken into account:

* The time of collection, quantity, temperature, sell-by dates and destination of the goods on a daily basis.

* The quantity of goods of each description in store properly rotated to ensure compliance with sell-by dates and identifying the rack location of each pallet to facilitate inventory control and quality assurance.

* The consolidation of orders for each RDC of each supermarket for delivery that night with orders being received between 2 p.m. and 6 p.m. and the consolidation of other loads for non-RDCs and hubs.

* The picking of orders from different pallets and the consequent repacking and shrink-wrapping of part or full pallets.

* The provision of vehicles and drivers to match an unpredictable demand which changes every day so with deliveries are made at specified times which permit no more than half an hour's leeway either way.

* The control and accounting for the pallets on which the goods are carried in respect of every collection or delivery.

* The control of drivers' hours and vehicle MOT checks and statistics.

* The correct and rapid invoicing of customers.

* The collection and processing of Proof of Delivery (POD) notes.

* The correlation of return loads.

* The investigation and settlement of claims.

* Especially where food is concerned, compliance with myriad regulations and controls, including the keeping of up-to-date records.

There are more variables, but that list indicates that we are dealing with a control problem of some complexity and one which was incapable of solution within the required time-scale prior to the application of computers to management control in the transport and distribution industry. I saw how it works in practice when I called in at Walford Cross immediately after lunch on the Monday after Christmas in 1998. It was a public holiday. Michael Donoghue, Rob Swindells, Paul Rowe, Chris Murt, Arran Osman and other managers were not working that day. When I arrived there was not much going on nor were the staff expecting much more activity later. Yet between 11.00 in the morning and 4.00 in the afternoon, direct delivery requests from RDCs arrived which involved selecting 1,381 pallets which in turn involved dispatching 116 vehicles that evening. None of the staff seemed surprised that all the deliveries were made correctly and on time, nor, it transpired, were the customers.

Christopher Murt (left) and Trevor Horton (right).

Most revelations do not happen on the road to Damascus. Langdons became more aware of the value of collecting and consolidating part-loads for concentration and next-day delivery when it became involved in a consortium known as Palletways. Under this scheme, hauliers were allocated postal districts to service from which they collected pallets of ambient goods for delivery next day anywhere in the United Kingdom, and trunked them each evening to a clearing warehouse in the Midlands. The trunker carried back pallets for delivery in his allocated area and the cycle operated as set out in the model above. The loss of the Taunton Cider work meant that Langdons no longer had the volume traffic to sustain its membership of Palletways, but that concept is a good one, and equally applicable to temperature-controlled work, if more difficult to introduce than where only dry goods are being handled.

The Gerber Foods business added another piece to the puzzle, with its requirement for daily delivery to all the RDCs. Obviously not every load would achieve the optimum of 24 pallets—weight considerations cut the number down from 26—and there was a virtue in filling the empty capacity with loads going to the same destination. This benefited everyone: the main customer by keeping the rate low, the customer with small loads on an *ad hoc* basis who could rely on a scheduled service, and the public through a more efficient use of vehicles.

Owing to other capital commitments Langdons were not in a position in the mid-1990s to establish the other strategic hubs necessary for the development of this business. This left it with two options: it could let the company be taken over by a national firm in the same business, or it could form strategic alliances with like-minded companies after the pattern of Palletways. The difficulty with the latter solution was that there were few independent like-minded companies with similar facilities with whom an alliance might be formed, and who could be relied on to give the standard of service which Langdons deemed necessary.

At that juncture Michael Donoghue received an approach from a quoted haulier already offering a service for chilled goods like the Palletways operation, but lacking a hub in the West Country. Companies like Langdons are always receiving offers from serious prospective buyers as well as carpetbaggers, but this proposal seemed to have the

merit of benefiting both the buyer and its target, although the Board of Langdons were
not happy about the other company's preference for hiring equipment rather than
buying it. The four owners of Langdons' shares agreed a price orally with the Managing
Director of the other firm and a meeting was arranged in the offices of its merchant
bankers in London to carry the transaction forward. I went to this meeting with
Michael Donoghue, our shoes buffed by the thick pile on the carpets on the top floor
for all the world as if the bank had not just lost £800 million through fraud, gambling,
negligence, poor supervision or greed in Singapore. We were given a cup of coffee after
which the three men on the other side of the table said they wanted to talk about the
price. Michael Donoghue folded up his papers, thanked them for their cup of coffee
and led me out of the room. The meeting lasted under 15 minutes, of which ten were
taken up by the ritual of obtaining and pouring drinks.

Langdons were to find out shortly afterwards that the proposed purchaser had
agreed to buy another haulage and distribution firm which, unlike Langdons, was strong
on profits based largely on a single contract, but weak on assets. The deal involved a
huge goodwill write-off and, when the principal contract was not renewed, our bidder
found itself under such difficulty that its share price fell and its own independent
existence became unsustainable. That in turn involved it abandoning the chilled-con-
solidation business, whereupon many of its customers transferred their business to Langdons
and to its old friend, Tom Granby, the firm which had rented the Arnos C warehouse
in Bristol. There are benefits, Langdons reflected, in owning kit rather than hiring it,
even if you grow more slowly as a result.

The solution of selling out to a national operator having proved incapable of
achievement—and indeed none of the shareholders had been very keen on it anyway—
Langdons were faced with establishing a series of hubs with like-minded firms to
provide a comprehensive service throughout the United Kingdom. The relationship
with Tom Granby, and in particular with its Managing Director Michael Redmond,
had been strengthened by the involvement of WMAS in negotiations to buy the
business from its Irish owner, although no deal was struck because the terms were at
that time too onerous, and Michael Redmond was able to do a better deal unaided a
few years later. It was agreed that Tom Granby would give up its warehouse in
Avonmouth, handing over all its west-of-England traffic to Langdons, while Langdons
would use Tom Granby's facilities in Merseyside and Luton for servicing appropriate
traffic to the north west and the south east. The business was established under the
trade-name Chillnet, which Langdons registered, and a Chillnet logo appeared on the
doors of all their vehicles. Other like-minded independent hauliers became involved to
provide daily coverage to all parts of the United Kingdom with a promise of next-day
delivery other than to Ireland.

The system is not perfect, because not all the parties involved can achieve the same
standards which Langdons sets itself, standards which were recognised in 1998 when the
leading supermarket chain in the United Kingdom in an internal document listed
Langdons as its most reliable haulier. All hauliers experience difficulties arising from the
traffic congestion and labour shortage in the Home Counties: nor is Liverpool an ideal
site in the north-west, being too far to the west of the spine motorway, the M6. That
said, within three years of its inauguration, the Chillnet business grew at Walford Cross
from an initial traffic of 50 pallets a day to something over 600 and by January 2000
Langdons were carrying between 6,000 and 9,000 pallets a week nationwide. Further

growth had for a time been constrained by a shortage of sub-zero storage space at Walford Cross, and that became available in September 1999. Rob Swindells was happy to have sold all the new capacity before the store opened, but unhappy that Langdons remained unable to accommodate any more of the business which was on offer.

Despite all his good works, Michael Donoghue will tell you that he is not in business for charitable purposes. It is therefore fortuitous that the establishment of Chillnet, with its guaranteed next-day delivery for anything from one pallet upwards on a published tariff, has opened up markets for smaller producers of dairy products and chilled and frozen foodstuffs which they were unable previously to reach. The resulting benefit to the rural economy of the south west in particular has been both real and lasting. Small producers can now make long-term commitments to large retailers knowing that their deliveries will be made, and at what cost. Similarly, national retailers know that they can depend on their smaller suppliers for the same service as they expect from larger companies. Even the ecologists should rejoice, with fewer vehicles carrying more traffic, although I don't suppose it will stop them, or journalists, continuing to use the pejorative and inaccurate 'juggernaut' when they mean 'articulated vehicle'.

Bessie Langdon built her business on the concept of getting dairy produce from small businesses on to the national market at a reasonable cost on a regular basis. Chillnet does not yet form the main part of the modern Langdons' business but it is growing apace, despite the emergence of competition, and one day perhaps it will be seen to perform as valuable and thorough a service for all parts of the United Kingdom economy, and for that of Ireland, as it does at present for the south west.

When Chillnet started, Langdons operated two temperature-controlled rigid vehicles to service the collection and delivery of goods within the south-west hub. By the spring of 2000, it was dedicating sixty vehicles to the same service nationally, apart from the rest of its fleet. Each of these sixty trucks is likely to be collecting and carrying the output of several producers, and, on its outward trip, making deliveries on behalf of several others. The saving of vehicle journeys compared with producers using their own transport or running one way in livery is as significant in its way as the saving by operating trunking to other regional hubs. The more Langdons' Chillnet lorries you see on the roads, the less the overall traffic. In addition, for those who cherish our countryside, the service enables producers in small towns and villages to compete with larger city-based operations, and so provide work locally. Many words are spoken in this sense by politicians and ecologists, but, as they say, action speaks louder than words.

In August 1999 Michael Donoghue and Rob Swindells concluded an arrangement for a hub in southern Ireland, bringing virtually the whole of the British Isles into the Chillnet scheme. The Irish agreement has the added attraction that Langdons' vehicles are able to buy diesel fuel some 20 pence a litre more cheaply on their trips across the water. The Irish government has a greater understanding of transport economics than its counterpart in Westminster and Whitehall; it realises the effect which punitive taxation on a basic service has on the cost of living and on the economy as a whole.

The only area in Britain in which small producers will continue to be denied the equal access to all United Kingdom markets afforded by Chillnet is the fertile agricultural district south of the Moray Firth; there a combination of remoteness and the fuel taxes levied by a Chancellor of the Exchequer, who happens to be Scottish, place disproportionate transport costs on local producers and so restrict the markets for their produce.

Twenty-Two

Why Langdons Stays British but Grew Away from Taunton Deane

You may recall that the compensation for the loss of the Arnos C temperature-controlled warehouse in Bristol financed for Langdons the conversion of an existing warehouse at Walford Cross for the storage of chilled fruit juices manufactured by Gerber Foods in Bridgwater, some seven miles down the road. Gerber's business grew rapidly and with it their demand for space at Langdons because all the production was trunked immediately to Walford Cross as it came off the line, rather than being held in Bridgwater. The storage requirement quickly outgrew the original warehouse conversion and bit by bit the remainder of the ambient storage space at Walford Cross was incorporated into the temperature-controlled part, until only the garage and Truck Stop remained.

The Walford Cross site had its problems, as does any commercial property where a firm is trying to expand and create more wealth for the good of the community and, of course, for its proprietors. Industrial expansion nearly always carries with it the inevitable penalty of increased traffic and perhaps noise or another form of nuisance. The frustrations which beset Taunton Cider in its prosperous days at Norton Fitzwarren were not unusual, especially in so environmentally-aware and caring a community as the Borough of Taunton Deane, which makes up for its underspending on security in its streets by night and in its car-parks by day through its exemplary vigilance in all matters relating to private nuisance or planning amenity.

One recurring complaint at Walford Cross comes from the neighbouring residents who are sensitive to noise, and especially that of vehicle-borne refrigeration equipment. As previously mentioned, there are adjoining the industrial site two houses originally built for its staff which TKM forbore to buy when it acquired the rest of the property. Although fronting on a trunk road and overlooking a motorway, changes in the law entitle the occupants to be free to open their bedroom windows on summer nights without the nuisance of being able to hear, and perhaps be kept awake by, the sound generated by industrial activity nearby. We must sympathise with the environmental officer whose duties compelled him to crouch with his recording apparatus in the hedge at the bottom of the garden anxiously counting his decibels, and with his superiors for whom the strict enforcement of the regulations may have seemed not quite what our legislators intended, if it involved in effect blighting three acres of an industrial site which had been used for that purpose for half a century. Reasonable compromises are reached eventually, after which Langdons' staff can also sleep peacefully at nights without the fear of losing their jobs.

Foul drainage was a more intractable problem because the nearest public sewer to Walford Cross is in Creech Heathfield, some distance the other side of the M5 motorway. The expansion of Langdons' transport operations meant that more lorries had to be washed (to comply with Food Hygiene regulations apart from aesthetics) and more oil and diesel fuel became mixed up with surface water. Then there was the Truck Stop which constantly placed greater demands on the septic tanks than they had been designed to carry. A stream ran off the site, passing through a farmer's land on the other side of the motorway, his sharp eye detecting, and his amanuensis reporting to the authorities,

A Langdons' 44-tonne articulated temperature-controlled rig in 2000.

any impurity in the water as it flowed by. The dilemma would have easier to resolve if the pollution in the stream came only from the Langdons' site: other contributors were the septic tanks of the two adjacent houses, a car breaker's yard, an agricultural machinery business, and the run-off from a trunk road.

The condition of the water in the stream ceased to give concern after Langdons, following the example of the Prince of Wales at Highgrove, constructed a reed bed through which all the outflow passed after treatment. For reasons which I am sure they would explain if pressed, the inspectors from the National Rivers Authority decided to switch their sampling of water to a point above the reed bed rather than test the crystal-clear fluid emerging below it. I suppose if you are paid to find something wrong and want to stay in business, you have to reach decisions of this kind.

The rational solution for the disposal of effluent would be to connect the outfall to the public sewer, which in this case would involve obtaining permission to pass through a culvert under the motorway and buying an easement from the farmer. The buying of the easement was a straightforward transaction, involving a few thousand pounds, some lawyers' fees and little delay. The Highway Authority, conscious of the benefit to society of solving the drainage problem, agreed readily to the passage of a pipe through the culvert, and referred the matter to the Ministry of Transport and the Treasury Solicitor. The months passed. Finally, when the Treasury Solicitor had cleared his or her desk sufficiently for this transaction to reach the top of the pile, someone in Brussels decided that all bridges and culverts must be tested to see if they would carry vehicles of up to 44 tonnes. As you may imagine, such was the load on the local authority highway engineers entrusted with this work that it was impossible to say how many years it might be before the culvert was declared capable of bearing the burden of having a pipe laid in it in addition to the existing stream. Until that survey was completed, there could no question of granting permission for Langdons to use the culvert. Eventually Langdons threw their hand in and the foul drainage still passes through the septic tanks and the clear water still comes out of the reed beds and the officials from the National Rivers Authority still come and take their samples from above the reed bed when the spirit moves them.

The Gerber business grew, and alongside it the Chillnet operation, requiring constantly more chilled pallet space and more equipment. In 1996 Langdons added a major extension to the warehouse, blocking both the view from the adjacent houses and stilling any lingering noise from the vehicle compressors, but without stilling the complaints to the local authority from the neighbours. This building, costing some £800,000, was commissioned a week early and would have come in on budget had it not been for the belated decision of a fire officer to request two-hour fire-proofing of one of the walls overlooking some green fields. This decision, which involved an additional expenditure of £16,000, did not appear to be in line with the relevant Building Regulations but appeals against such rulings take about 18 months to resolve, during which time it would have been impossible to obtain a Fire Certificate, and so insurance, for the building. It is comforting to reflect that sheep in the adjoining pastures may safely graze without any risk to their fleeces should the building go up in smoke, having two hours in which to move out of harm's way.

In 1997 the international manufacturer, Procter and Gamble, decided to undertake test marketing in the north of England of its chilled fruit drink called *Sunny Delight*, already a big seller in the Americas. Procter and Gamble have grown into one of the largest and most successful companies in the world through developing saleable products such as soap powders and through finding new markets for the products which they have already developed, as with the nappy-liners called *Pampers*. Every activity which they undertake is planned and controlled in meticulous detail, the distribution of a product having no less attention than its development, manufacture and marketing. Because of the reputation both firms had gained for quality and reliability, Gerber Foods were chosen for the trial manufacture of *Sunny Delight* and Langdons for the distribution. At first it seemed quite a small job, with reports coming through that the good folks of Cumbria found *Sunny Delight* to their liking.

Following the successful test-marketing, Procter and Gamble decided in the summer of 1997 to introduce *Sunny Delight* throughout the United Kingdom, and again asked Langdons to undertake the storage, picking and distribution, which involved providing spaces for 5,000 pallets under chilled conditions, and equipment to deliver up to a hundred loads a day. Langdons was then to discover that Procter and Gamble conduct their affairs with a professionalism and openness which had not been apparent in previous dealings with, for example, the manufacturers of cider. Still smarting from the Hartcliffe experience, Michael Donoghue asked for and was given a five-year exclusive contract for the storage and picking of the product, with a year guaranteed for transport. In return, to provide the storage space, Langdons needed to build another new warehouse at Walford Cross, with many more loading bays, and to do that it had to pull down the Truck Stop and the garage. Another problem was the timing, as the warehouse had to be operational by 1 March 1998. A third difficulty was over cash.

The four original partners, Michael Donoghue, Rob Swindells, Paul Rowe, and WMAS, had adopted a rule that they would not let Langdons borrow, whether from the bank or through hire purchase, more in total than the amount of their equity. As they had established other rules that the firm would always buy equipment rather than rent it, and occupy freehold property rather than leaseholds, this had had the effect of restricting the company's growth. Conversely, as we saw, it enabled it to emerge relatively undamaged from the loss of the Taunton Cider business. To build and equip the new store and buy the additional tractors and trailers to service the Procter and Gamble contract required an equity injection into the business of £1.5 million if the self-imposed guidelines were to be observed.

A number of local businessmen and women had enquired from time to time if there might be an opportunity of investing in Langdons. Michael Donoghue now told them that the moment had arrived. Furthermore WMAS had recently ceased to be involved in a manufacturing business in Leeds where, for 14 years or so, a significant investor, the publicly-quoted Majedie Investments plc through its Managing Director William Underwood, had proved stalwart—interested and helpful but not anxious, impatient or interfering. The Rix family, headed by the shrewd analyst John Rix, had also invested in the Leeds business and similarly shown that it understood that growth is something which has to be planned and developed, and does not usually happen overnight. Both these parties were invited to subscribe for Langdons' shares.

It did not prove difficult to arrange for the subscription of the required £1.5 million without having to approach strangers, and Michael was also gratified when Christopher Murt and Rupert Ryall, the two managers who had been subjected to the diligent but misguided attention of the Wiltshire constabulary, asked to become significant shareholders. As often happens, when some of those who had suggested a figure which they wished to invest had spoken to their advisers, they had second thoughts: it is naturally hard for an adviser to express a view if he is not retained to underwrite the issue, although the fact that he would not be receiving any commission would naturally never be allowed to colour such advice. Other investors introduced by Peter Moore, the Taunton stockbroker who couples a keen investment brain with constant support for local industry and employment, soon filled the gap and the only query raised by any prospective investor was why the issue price was not at a premium to the company's assets. The answer was that the directors wished to be selective as to the parties they invited to join them in the ownership of Langdons.

The share issue meant that the holding of the original team fell to 72 per cent of the equity, at which level they could not force through any change to the Articles of Association against the wishes of the outside shareholders, but they could continue to protect the company from unwanted predators. To ensure that the new investors had full and independent information about the business, due diligence was undertaken by the company's auditors, which included the revaluation of its freehold property. The total cost of the new issue, including professional fees and stamp duties, came to just under £15,000, or less than 1 per cent of the money raised.

To provide further protection for the outside investors, it was decided to ask two non-executive members to join the board. Wilf Dickinson, the talented refrigeration engineer who advises Langdons and is also an investor, was a natural candidate, but his appointment in a non-executive role would have meant that he would not be free to perform a continuing executive function. Langdons could not afford to lose that important asset.

When the Leeds company in which Majedie invested had been bought out of receivership in 1982, the merchant banker Richard Cox-Johnson, the financial advisers Larpent Newton, and WMAS had all been involved. The story of how the team saw off an American over-bidder is fascinating, but will have to be told elsewhere, if at all. The company prospered and I had been happy to remain associated with it as its Chairman, while WMAS remained a significant investor.

When this company was sold in 1996, the Chairman and Managing Director lost their jobs, as is to be expected on such occasions. The Chairman's grief was assuaged in part by the fact that the investment by WMAS had increased by a factor of something over five times during the previous decade, while the Managing Director's initial investment had multiplied by a factor of twenty-four. Between them Majedie, the Rix family and WMAS owned some 25 per cent or more of the company, which was enough to block the sale. William Underwood and John Rix were satisfied with the sale price but they were unhappy to observe when they received the documentation that, although the Managing Director was being generously compensated for his loss of office, the Chairman was receiving nothing: indeed they were so unhappy that they said they would not support the sale until what they saw as an injustice was remedied. I reminded them, as you have already been told, that it was not the policy of WMAS to seek any security or entitlement to compensation for loss of office when accepting a continuing role in a client company. They had also to understand that, when it comes to generosity in dispensing cash, Yorkshiremen have a reputation to live down to. However the solicitude and sense of fair play shown by William Underwood and John Rix, coupled with their past record as investors, induced me to suggest that they be invited to become Langdons' first non-executive directors, as indeed they did and are.

As the sales of *Sunny Delight* grew, so it became evident that the refrigerated space at Walford Cross was not enough. The need was now for 10,000 pallet storage to service the volume being manufactured in Bridgwater. Michael Donoghue was naturally anxious not to run a split operation on two sites in the same area, and entered into negotiations with a neighbouring farmer to buy land on which an additional warehouse could be built. Sensing perhaps that Langdons needed the site urgently and that there was no alternative land available, the farmer's agent asked for considerably more money per acre than he had not long before charged a neighbouring caravan distributor for fields adjoining. The land was not ideal for building, being blighted by electricity pylons overhead and a main gas pipeline underneath. To shield any development from the motorway alongside, a large part of the site would have to be given over to landscaping, further increasing the usable cost per acre. Then there were the inevitable planning and highway objections.

The site was not designated for industrial development, but then almost no land in the Borough of Taunton Deane is. There was talk of relocating the cattle market in the vicinity and an expansion of the caravan distributorship had recently been agreed. Apart, however, from the landscaping requirement, there was the dreaded Section 106 threat. This provision is intended to enable local authorities recover from a developer a contribution towards the cost of any additional public services necessitated through the development. In practice, it can be used as blackmail.

Procter and Gamble required the new facility by 1 June 1999. To have any hope of meeting the deadline, Langdons had to apply for planning permission, paying the council a fee of £9,500, no later than 7 September 1998, a date determined by the deliberations of the Planning Committees and their advisers. This fee was additional to the £18,000 or so the firm had already spent on various consultants without whose advice no major planning application is likely to receive serious consideration. That day Michael Donoghue happened to be on a course, although which hole he was playing when I reached Walford Cross has not been recorded. I spoke to Kenneth Steel, the talented architect who has designed all Langdons' buildings and was liaising with the planners. He told me that a fresh concern had been raised which would involve paying £12,500 for an archaeological survey before any building could commence. If archaeological remains were found, the ensuing delay would be unpredictable.

Meanwhile the other WMAS director on the Langdons' board, my son Rob Holder, had obtained details of a 10-acre site in Bridgwater which already had planning permission at what amounted to much the same price per acre as that which the farmer was asking, closer to the M5 motorway, with no Section 106 threat, no archaeological survey, no excessive landscaping. In addition Sedgemoor District Council is more sympathetic than Taunton Deane to job creation other than in the public sector, and encourages properly controlled industrial development. I was pondering these matters when, having no office of my own at Langdons, I walked into Michael Donoghue's to draft some Heads of Agreement which Procter and Gamble had asked me to prepare for the new contract.

I was surprised to find Rob Swindells sitting there with the three senior executives from Procter and Gamble who had flown in from Hamburg to see Gerber, a visit of which Langdons had had no prior notice. They explained that the new capacity had to be available by 1 June 1999. It was clear that there was no hope of achieving this so long as we persevered with the local farmer, his agent and the Taunton planners. I explained that we would need some capital assistance if we went ahead immediately with the Bridgwater site. They asked how much. I mentioned a sum well into seven figures. They looked at each other for a moment, and then the senior man in the party nodded, and said that this was not a problem. In the event the subvention turned out to be 50 per cent higher than what I had suggested, but that was no problem either.

Michael Donoghue returned from his annual day-out the following morning and immediately endorsed the decisions Rob Swindells and I had taken. The Taunton planners were somewhat miffed that we had not pursued the option at Walford Cross, their keenness for our proposals in retrospect contrasting oddly with their previous caution. Kenneth Steel and Wilf Dickinson went ahead with the Bridgwater site, which became operational on 1 June 1999. A few days later Langdons took over the operation of another logistics facility for Gerber/Procter and Gamble in Blackburn. (I was amused to observe that Wilf, in the Bridgwater building, placed an extractor fan in a fire door as the deliberate mistake for the Fire Officer to pick up. By doing that, securing a Fire Certificate cost £200 in rectification works, against the wasted £16,000 at Walford Cross.)

As I write, Langdons has three warehouse and transport sites—Walford Cross, Bridgwater, and Blackburn—and in addition operates out of Knowsley and Luton. It has

Langdons' warehouse, garage, and offices in Bridgwater.

two main sources of business—logistics for firms such as Gerber and Procter and Gamble, and Chillnet. It currently employs around 350 men and women and through its personnel assessment programmes the company is always on the lookout for younger people who can be trained to take on management roles, in the knowledge that the old guard cannot and should not continue indefinitely. Although the long years of transition from loss to modest profits to rapid growth have seen the risks taken by the original buy-out team justified and their fortunes grow, none of them has any desire to become any richer at the risk of jeopardising the livelihood of so many dedicated and loyal men and women who have turned Langdons into one of the most efficient and highly respected hauliers in the country. In July 1999, despite the disruption of the two major moves which it had just completed, Langdons was named as the top performer of all logistics firms used by Procter and Gamble, with 70,000 deliveries made without a single one being missed.

The derelict site of Taunton Cider plc in nearby Norton Fitzwarren remains a constant reminder that security lies in independence. As we saw, what was once Taunton Cider is now the subsidiary of an American parent, along with Matthew Clark and the various other brands which were household names. Nearly all the Norton Fitzwarren employees lost their jobs. Another Taunton company which we have mentioned, James Pearsall, passed out of local and British control in August 1999 when it too became the subsidiary of an American parent. Then on 21 September 1999 Avimo, the company which I contracted to buy from Henri Feuillée on a single sheet of paper in 1966 for £330,000, was sold by its parent to a French buyer for £58.4 million. Perhaps I should have retained my 12.5 per cent share: but, no, it's only money and as M. Feuillée said to me on many occasions *Ne regrette rien*. With its return to French ownership, the Avimo wheel also has come full circle.

There is a film clip taken immediately after the Matthew Clark take-over of Taunton Cider was announced in which Peter Adams and two of his colleagues are seen smiling as they are walking and talking to the media. No, there would not be any redundancies at Norton Fitzwarren. The first duty the directors had, said Mr. Adams, was to their employees. In fact, directors have several complementary duties: to their shareholders, to their customers, to their employees, to their suppliers, to their country, to their local community, and to their families. Whatever has been the fate of other major industrial enterprises based in Taunton, Michael Donoghue, Rob Swindells, and Paul Rowe have achieved the right balance in their stewardship of Langdons.

Michael Donoghue sitting at his desk with, from left, Paul Rowe, Sheila Burnett, Rupert Ryall and Rob Swindells.

EPILOGUE

On 1 December 1999 Langdons took over all the transport operations of Tom Granby (Liverpool) Ltd, which increased the Langdons' Chillnet fleet by some fifty vehicles, the majority of which are rigid trucks suitable for small drops. Langdons now has lorries based at all three hubs, in Luton, in Merseyside, and in Somerset. With this nationally-based fleet, the company offers manufacturers of temperature-controlled products anywhere in the United Kingdom (other than Ireland) an access to national markets which was not previously available because of the cost and uncertainty of the transport of part loads. The need for this service to smaller firms has already been demonstrated in south-west England, where the daily volume of Chillnet pallets through Walford Cross is nudging a thousand.

As anticipated, the former Taunton Cider site at Norton Fitzwarren became ear-marked for residential use, although many locals objected to that just as they had to any industrial development proposed by the cider company. The *Taunton Cider* brand has been retained by its new owners and the cider still tastes the same despite being made elsewhere.

In his spring budget, the Chancellor of the Exchequer again increased the duty of diesel but abandoned the ratchet formula which had already made British hauliers unable to compete with their Irish and continental competitors for international traffic. The Government continued to deplore the economic 'divide' between the south-east and other parts of the Kingdom, without acknowledging that its fiscal regime, through taxing remoteness, was throwing fuel on the flames. It continued its avowed policy of reducing the administrative burden on companies by issuing upwards of 3,000 fresh Regulations within a period of twelve months.

In April 2000, the leading cider. manufacturer, H.P. Bulmer, announced that its turnover in 1999 had reached £315 million, although its profits, at £24 million, remained at the level achieved in 1996 before the impact of Alcopops. In contrast to Taunton Cider which (as we saw) had been bought by a company largely engaged in distribution, Bulmer had bought its own drinks distributor, Dawes Group, for £32 million.

In March 2000, Fox Brothers, the venerable textile manufacturers in Wellington, and formerly also in Wiveliscombe, founded in the 18th century and at one time employing up to 3,000 people, went into receivership. The following month a man-agement team acquired the assets from the Receiver without revealing how many jobs would be created in the new company.

In April, 2000 the Wellington bedding company Relyon, announced forty job losses.

By May, 2000, the Euro had continued sinking in value against sterling and the dollar, losing almost all its British supporters other than the BBC, for which the operation of any free market remains anathema, lest its own monopoly and wastefulness might be questioned. The flood of politically correct, but economically damaging, judgments and rules from Brussels and Strasbourg continued to erode the will of the

British public to surrender its sovereignty to continental bureaucrats and jurists, raising the spectre that Westminster might again house a sovereign parliament, and failed politicians might no longer have the prospect of a retirement cushioned by a tax-free berth in Brussels.

INDEX

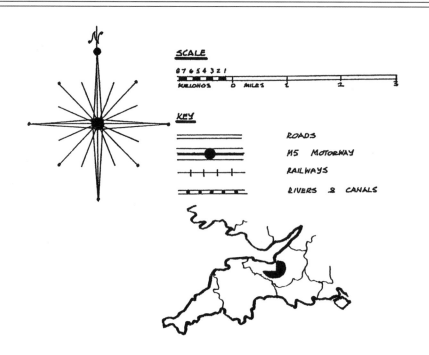

SCALE

8 7 6 5 4 3 2 1

KILOMETRES 0 MILES 1 2 3

KEY

─────── ROADS

━━●━━━ M5 MOTORWAY

─┼─┼─┼─ RAILWAYS

▭▭▭▭▭ RIVERS & CANALS

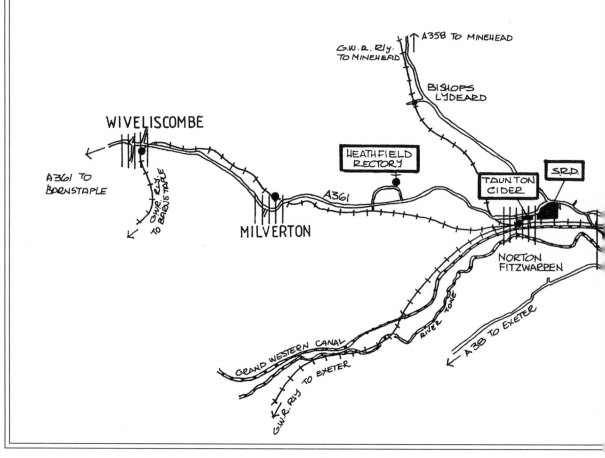

A358 TO MINEHEAD

G.W.R. Rly. TO MINEHEAD

BISHOPS LYDEARD

WIVELISCOMBE

HEATHFIELD RECTORY

TAUNTON CIDER

S.P.D.

A361 TO BARNSTAPLE

G.W.R. Rly. TO BARNSTAPLE

A361

MILVERTON

NORTON FITZWARREN

GRAND WESTERN CANAL

G.W.R. Rly. TO EXETER

RIVER TONE

A38 TO EXETER